Scott Foresman

Scott Foresman

Editorial Offices: Glenview, Illinois • Parsippany, New Jersey • New York, New York
Sales Offices: Parsippany, New Jersey • Duluth, Georgia • Glenview, Illinois
Coppell, Texas • Ontario, California

Credits

Illustrations

Teresa Anderko: pp. 2, 58, 82, 149, 162, 260; **Nelle Davis:** pp. 7, 22, 32, 38, 42, 52, 77, 92, 102, 112, 127, 132, 138, 147, 152, 222, 228; **Waldo Dunn:** pp. 192, 238, 242, 252, 278; **Vickie Learner:** p. 89; **Mapping Specialists:** pp. 221, 223, 229; **Laurie O'Keefe:** pp. 39, 129, 239, 240, 299; **Joel Snyder:** pp. 72, 78; **TSI Graphics:** pp. 19, 29, 30, 59, 60, 69, 70, 109, 119, 179, 232, 248, 260, 292; **N. Jo Tufts:** pp. 18, 118, 142, 158, 212; **Jessica Wolk-Stanley:** pp. 179, 259.

ISBN: 0-328-02248-9
ISBN: 0-328-04052-5

13 14 V011 10 09 08
13 14 V011 10 09

Table of Contents

Unit 4

Timeless Stories

	Comprehension	Vocabulary	Selection Test	Phonics/ Word Study	Research and Study Skills
Half-Chicken	151, 153, 157	152	155–156	158	159–160
Blame It on the Wolf	161, 163, 167	162	165–166	168	169–170
Lou Gehrig: The Luckiest Man	171, 173, 177	172	175–176	178	179–180
The Disguise	181, 183, 187	182	185–186	188	189–190
Keepers	191, 193, 197	192	195–196	198	199–200

Unit 5

Other Times, Other Places

	Comprehension	Vocabulary	Selection Test	Phonics/ Word Study	Research and Study Skills
Amazing Alice!	201, 203, 207	202	205–206	208	209–210
A Peddler's Dream	211, 213, 217	212	215–216	218	219–220
The Race for the North Pole	221, 223, 227	222	225–226	228	229–230
Into the Sea	231, 233, 237	232	235–236	238	239–240
Space Probes to the Planets	241, 243, 247	242	245–246	248	249–250

Unit 6

Express Yourself!

	Comprehension	Vocabulary	Selection Test	Phonics/ Word Study	Research and Study Skills
Koya's Cousin Del	251, 253, 257	252	255–256	258	259–260
Children of Clay	261, 263, 267	262	265–266	268	269–270
Coming Home	271, 273, 277	272	275–276	278	279–280
Out of the Blue	281, 283, 287	282	285–286	288	289–290
Chocolate Is Missing	291, 293, 297	292	295–296	298	299–300

Setting

- **Setting** is the time and place in which a story occurs.
- Sometimes pictures show the setting, and sometimes you have to visualize it from details the author has written.

Directions: Reread this passage from "A Visit with Grandpa" and try to visualize the scene it paints. Then answer the questions below.

Now the sun heated up the morning. The foothills were now varying shades of green. Shadows dotted the plains. Among the blackish green trees on the rolling hills, fog still lingered like lazy clouds. Insects buzzed. A small cloud of mosquitoes swarmed just behind their heads, and beautiful cardinals splashed their redness on the morning air. Justin felt a surge of happiness and hugged Black with his knees and heels.

From JUSTIN AND THE BEST BISCUITS IN THE WORLD by Mildred Pitts Walter. Text Copyright © 1986 by Mildred Pitts Walter. By permission of Lothrop, Lee & Shepard Books, a division of William Morrow & Company, Inc.

1. What season of the year do you think it is? Why?

_____

_____

2. What can you tell about the time in which the story takes place? Explain.

_____

_____

3. What colors and sounds does Justin see and hear?

_____

_____

4. Why do you think Justin feels a "surge of happiness"?

_____

5. Use a separate sheet of paper to describe a place that makes you feel the way Justin does. Remember to include vivid details about the setting.

Notes for Home: Your child has read a story and used story details to visualize its setting.
Home Activity: Have your child describe in detail a place both of you know well. Then try to guess the place. Take turns describing and guessing other places.

Name_____

1.	Ⓐ	Ⓑ	Ⓒ	Ⓓ
2.	Ⓕ	Ⓖ	Ⓗ	Ⓙ
3.	Ⓐ	Ⓑ	Ⓒ	Ⓓ
4.	Ⓕ	Ⓖ	Ⓗ	Ⓙ
5.	Ⓐ	Ⓑ	Ⓒ	Ⓓ
6.	Ⓕ	Ⓖ	Ⓗ	Ⓙ
7.	Ⓐ	Ⓑ	Ⓒ	Ⓓ
8.	Ⓕ	Ⓖ	Ⓗ	Ⓙ
9.	Ⓐ	Ⓑ	Ⓒ	Ⓓ
10.	Ⓕ	Ⓖ	Ⓗ	Ⓙ
11.	Ⓐ	Ⓑ	Ⓒ	Ⓓ
12.	Ⓕ	Ⓖ	Ⓗ	Ⓙ
13.	Ⓐ	Ⓑ	Ⓒ	Ⓓ
14.	Ⓕ	Ⓖ	Ⓗ	Ⓙ
15.	Ⓐ	Ⓑ	Ⓒ	Ⓓ

Textbook/Trade Book

Textbooks usually teach about one subject, such as social studies or math. These books are organized to help you find information quickly. Each **chapter title** tells you about a main section of the book, and the **headings** and **subheadings** show what information you can find in a particular section. **Vocabulary words** are often printed in bold and included in the margin.

Directions: Use the textbook section to answer the questions that follow.

CHAPTER 8 American History 1865–1885

A Cowboy's Life

Chefs on the Prairie

chuck wagon: vehicle that carried meals to cowboys

A cowboy's job involved many hours of hard work, so when dinnertime finally arrived, he was ready for hearty meals. Since cowboys used the word "chuck" to mean food, the vehicle that carried the food around was called a **chuck wagon.** These wagons, which also served as kitchens, hotels, and ranch headquarters, were driven by the cook.

Dutch oven: a large, heavy kettle

The cook's day began at about 3:00 A.M. He would wake up the crew to help him prepare breakfast. Some cowboys complained that they had to work from sunrise to sunset, or as they put it from "can't see to can't see." To bake the biscuits, the camp chefs used cast iron **Dutch ovens.** These ovens were used to bake biscuits, cornbread, fruit cobblers, and cakes. Popular cowboy meals around the campfire included beef, beans, biscuits, rice, and dried fruit. Cowboys rarely ate fresh vegetables, milk, or eggs.

1. How could you quickly find the definitions for vocabulary words on this page?

   _____

   _____

2. If you wanted to write an essay called "A Day in the Life of a Cowboy," do you think this textbook chapter would be helpful? Explain why or why not.

   _____

   _____

3. What part of the page tells you the time period this chapter covers?

   _____

   _____

A **trade book** is any book that is not a textbook, a periodical, or a reference book. The skills you use for understanding trade books are a lot like those you use when you read textbooks. When you choose a trade book, think about your purpose for reading, the same as you would for choosing a reference book.

Directions: Use the trade book excerpt to answer the questions that follow.

25

Chapter 3: If You Were a Wild West Wrangler

Q: Did cowboys travel with tables and chairs?

A: They usually ate their meals sitting or squatting on the ground.

Q: What other responsibilities did a cowboy cook have?

A: In addition to preparing food, it was not unusual for the cook to serve as the camp doctor and barber. The cook also drove the chuck wagon. Every night after dinner, the cook pointed the wagon toward the North Star, so he could head in the right direction the next day.

---

4. How is the information in this book organized? How might this be helpful for writing an essay about a cowboy's daily life?

_____

_____

5. In addition to cooking meals, what other responsibilities did the cook have?

_____

_____

Notes for Home: Your child used a textbook and a trade book to locate information and draw conclusions. ***Home Activity:*** Discuss some other resources your child might use to find information about cowboys, such as history TV channels, history magazines, and so on.

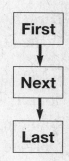

Sequence

- **Sequence** means the order in which things happen. **Sequence** can also mean steps we follow to do something.
- Clue words such as *first, then, next,* and *finally* help you figure out the sequence of events.
- Some events in a story may take place at the same time. Authors may use words like *meanwhile, while,* or *during* to show this.
- Sometimes events are told out of order. Verb tenses or clue words can show this.

First
↓
Next
↓
Last

Directions: Reread "Will Sarah Return?" On the lines below, write the story events from the box in the order that they happened. Use the letter shown next to each event.

Story Events

a. Anna sweeps the porch.

b. Anna sweeps the porch again.

c. Caleb picks up Seal.

d. Seal jumps onto the porch.

e. Anna asks her father where Sarah has gone.

f. Caleb cleans out the stove.

g. Anna watches a wagon take Mama away.

h. Caleb spills the ashes.

i. Anna and Caleb watch Sarah.

j. Anna and Caleb take lunch to their father.

---

1. _____

2. _____

3. _____

4. _____

5. _____

6. _____

7. _____

8. _____

9. _____

10. _____

Notes for Home: Your child read a story and identified the order in which the story events occurred. *Home Activity:* Work with your child to create a "My Day" list that shows all your child's activities in order from waking up in the morning to the present time.

Vocabulary

Directions: Choose the word from the box that best completes each sentence.
Write the word on the matching numbered line to the right.

Mr. and Mrs. Garcia are the **1.** _____ next
door. Last month they told me they were
going to **2.** _____ a daughter. Mrs. Garcia
took out her **3.** _____ and showed me the
country where the baby was born. She said
that she would be very happy to end the
4. _____ of waiting so long for the baby.
Yesterday I saw Mr. Garcia happily pushing
a **5.** _____ with a beautiful baby girl inside.

1. _____

2. _____

3. _____

4. _____

5. _____

Check the Words You Know
__ adopt
__ atlas
__ carriage
__ couple
__ misery
__ platform

Directions: Choose the word from the box that best matches each clue. Write the
word in the puzzle.

Down

6. accept a child of other parents and bring
   it up as your own
7. book of maps
9. great unhappiness

Across

8. a raised, level surface
10. a 4-wheeled vehicle that is pulled or pushed

Write a Story

On a separate sheet of paper, write a story about a couple who think
they are adopting a puppy, but get a very different kind of animal
instead. Use as many of the vocabulary words as you can.

Notes for Home: Your child identified and used new vocabulary words from *Train to
Somewhere*. **Home Activity:** With your child, make up a story about a child traveling to a new
home. Encourage your child to use as many of the vocabulary words as possible.

Name _____

Sequence

- **Sequence** means the order in which things happen. Clue words such as *first, then, next,* and *finally* help you figure out the sequence of events.
- Authors do not always use clue words to show sequence.

Directions: Reread what happens in *Train to Somewhere* after Marianne and eight other children leave the first stop, Porterville, Illinois. Then answer the questions below. Look for any clue words the author uses to show the sequence of events.

> Nine of us are left to get back on the train. Miss Randolph says we're to keep on our good clothes. We'll be getting off again soon.
>
> At Kilburn we are walked to a hardware store to stand in line.
>
> "I expect they took all the biggest boys in Porterville," one man says. "But still. . . ."
>
> Eddie Hartz, who is only seven, is taken. There's a boy who can stand on his hands and pretend to pull buttons out of people's ears. He makes the crowd laugh and he gets taken, too.
>
> As soon as the train has loaded on wood and fresh water, the rest of us get back aboard.
>
> Excerpt from TRAIN TO SOMEWHERE by Eve Bunting. Text copyright © 1996 by Eve Bunting. Reprinted by permission of Clarion Books/Houghton Mifflin Company. All rights reserved.

1. What is the first event of this passage? _____

_____

2. What is the last event of this passage? _____

_____

3. Were the children wearing their good clothes before they got to Kilburn? How do you know?

_____

4. How many children get back on the train? How do you know?

_____

5. On a separate sheet of paper, write three sentences telling what happens next in the story.

Notes for Home: Your child has read a story and used story details to describe the order in which events occurred. *Home Activity:* Have your child make a list of tomorrow's activities. Then ask him or her to number the list in the order that the events are expected to happen.

Name_____

1.	Ⓐ	Ⓑ	Ⓒ	Ⓓ
2.	Ⓕ	Ⓖ	Ⓗ	Ⓙ
3.	Ⓐ	Ⓑ	Ⓒ	Ⓓ
4.	Ⓕ	Ⓖ	Ⓗ	Ⓙ
5.	Ⓐ	Ⓑ	Ⓒ	Ⓓ
6.	Ⓕ	Ⓖ	Ⓗ	Ⓙ
7.	Ⓐ	Ⓑ	Ⓒ	Ⓓ
8.	Ⓕ	Ⓖ	Ⓗ	Ⓙ
9.	Ⓐ	Ⓑ	Ⓒ	Ⓓ
10.	Ⓕ	Ⓖ	Ⓗ	Ⓙ
11.	Ⓐ	Ⓑ	Ⓒ	Ⓓ
12.	Ⓕ	Ⓖ	Ⓗ	Ⓙ
13.	Ⓐ	Ⓑ	Ⓒ	Ⓓ
14.	Ⓕ	Ⓖ	Ⓗ	Ⓙ
15.	Ⓐ	Ⓑ	Ⓒ	Ⓓ

Selection Test

Directions: Choose the best answer to each item. Mark the letter for the answer you have chosen.

Part 1: Vocabulary

Find the answer choice that means about the same as the underlined word in each sentence.

1. Wanda described her <u>misery</u> to me.
   A. way of doing things
   B. great suffering or unhappiness
   C. adventure
   D. plans for the future

2. The <u>platform</u> is large and sturdy.
   F. a chest for clothing
   G. a wall made of stone
   H. a wooden box
   J. a raised flat surface

3. The Lees will <u>adopt</u> a little boy.
   A. have happy memories of
   B. raise a child of other parents as their own
   C. pay a visit to
   D. guide someone on a long trip

4. I borrowed this <u>atlas</u> from Arnie.
   F. small suitcase
   G. old-fashioned camera
   H. book of maps
   J. heavy jacket

5. The <u>carriage</u> needs to be repaired.
   A. something to carry passengers
   B. something to eat with
   C. something to train animals
   D. something to row with

6. The <u>couple</u> ate dinner at home.
   F. the children of a family
   G. several people who are traveling together
   H. a close relative
   J. two people with a close relationship

Part 2: Comprehension

Use what you know about the story to answer each item.

7. What is the first thing Marianne does each time the train stops?
   A. has some cookies and milk
   B. changes into old clothes
   C. tries to look pleasant
   D. looks for her mother in the crowd

8. Miss Randolph's feeling about the children is that they—
   F. are hard to care for.
   G. will all be happy in their new homes.
   H. are fussy and spoiled.
   J. are very special and she will miss them.

GO ON

9. Which event in this story happens before the train leaves New York?
- A. Nora and Marianne sit together on the train.
- B. Miss Randolph gives the children milk and cookies.
- C. Marianne's mother leaves her at St. Christopher's.
- D. The train stops at a town called Somewhere.

10. The feather Marianne carries in her pocket is a—
- F. reminder of her mother.
- G. gift from Nora.
- H. decoration for her hair.
- J. lucky charm.

11. How does Marianne feel when the train reaches Somewhere?
- A. peaceful and content
- B. tired and bored
- C. excited and hopeful
- D. hurt and unloved

12. What happens first when Marianne meets the Books?
- F. She gives Mrs. Book her feather.
- G. She notices that the Books are old.
- H. She agrees to go with the Books.
- J. She asks for a puppy.

13. Which sentence best describes the lesson in this story?
- A. Children should learn to do the things that please adults.
- B. Friends are usually more important than relatives.
- C. Sometimes what you get is better than what you wished for.
- D. Adults always know what is best for children.

14. Which sentence suggests that Marianne likes Mrs. Book?
- F. "She's wearing a heavy black dress and a man's droopy black hat."
- G. "The woman's holding a wooden toy locomotive."
- H. "Somehow this woman understands about me, how it felt that nobody wanted me."
- J. "She pats Mr. Book's hand and they smile at each other."

15. In this story, Marianne's biggest disappointment was—
- A. leaving Miss Randolph.
- B. leaving St. Christopher's.
- C. being taken by the Books.
- D. knowing her mother had not come for her.

Cause and Effect

Directions: Read the story. Then read each question about the story. Choose the best answer to each question. Mark the letter for the answer you have chosen.

Leaving Time

Mom told me that her family was always late leaving on vacation. That's because they didn't like to get up early. Also, it took a long time to get ready.

Mom said Grandma had too many clothes. She could never decide what to pack.

Grandpa always spotted a chore he forgot to do. Mom usually found him cleaning or fixing something. Sometimes he couldn't find the map.

My uncle David had hair that wouldn't stay down. He would spend an hour combing it. Then it would pop up again.

Mom could never decide what books to take. So she had to start reading each one.

1. Which was **not** a cause of the family leaving late?
   A. getting up late
   B. the weather
   C. Grandma's packing
   D. Mom's reading

2. What was the effect of David's hair not staying down?
   F. He forgot to comb it.
   G. He had a cowlick.
   H. His combing made the family late.
   J. His hair popped up.

3. What might Grandpa do to make the family late?
   A. go to the park
   B. comb his hair
   C. fix the lawn sprinkler
   D. eat a big breakfast

4. What might have helped the family be on time?
   F. eat breakfast together
   G. pack the night before
   H. check the weather report
   J. get gas for the car

5. In the following sentence, which word gives a clue about why something happened?
   David's hair wouldn't stay down, so he took a long time combing it.
   A. wouldn't
   B. down
   C. time
   D. so

 Notes for Home: Your child identified causes and effects in a story. *Home Activity:* Play a game of cause and effect. When something happens at home, look for causes and effects. For example, if the timer doesn't go off (cause), then dinner may burn (effect).

© Scott Foresman 4

Phonics: Vowel Digraphs

Directions: Read each sentence. Say the underlined word to yourself. Listen for the vowel sounds that the letters **ea** and **ou** represent in <u>**feather, peak,**</u> and <u>**country.**</u> Circle the word in ( ) that has the same vowel sound as the underlined word.

1. The <u>steam</u> train pulled into the station. (break/beat)

2. The train was taking orphan children to the <u>country</u>. (found/tough)

3. Many people had <u>read</u> about the children on the train. (sea/dead)

4. The train traveled in all kinds of <u>weather</u>. (bread/bead)

5. After four days, the children had had <u>enough</u> of riding the train. (though/tough)

6. Not knowing where their next home would be was <u>tough</u> on them. (fought/rough)

7. <u>Instead</u> of getting off the train, they waited until the next stop. (head/meat)

8. Only one <u>couple</u> came to meet the train at the stop. (rough/bought)

9. The woman had a white <u>feather</u> in her hat. (fear/head)

10. She quickly <u>reached</u> out to welcome the children. (seat/ready)

Directions: Read each word. Say it to yourself. Listen for the **vowel sound** that the underlined letters represent. Find the word with a different vowel spelling that has the same **vowel sound.** Circle the word.

11. c<u>ou</u>ntry	cold	foul	fun
12. w<u>ea</u>ther	bed	bath	bead
13. h<u>ea</u>t	height	receive	wait
14. c<u>ou</u>ple	cup	cope	cop
15. h<u>ea</u>ven	heave	seven	haven

© Scott Foresman 4

Research Process

Begin your research by asking yourself questions about your topic. Find resources, such as encyclopedias, that will help answer these questions. As you gather information, you can ask new questions. Summarize the information you find by taking notes or writing outlines. Then organize your information into a report.

Directions: Complete the table. For rows 1, 2, and 3, decide what key words would help you locate information in a reference source. For row 4, write a question based on the key word that you could answer in your research.

What I Want to Find Out	Key Words
What year did the first Orphan Train leave?	1.
How many people lived in New York City in 1880?	2.
Are any orphan-train riders alive today?	3.
4.	railroad

Directions: Use the information on this set of encyclopedias to answer the questions that follow.

5. Which volume would help you find out what year the helicopter was invented? Explain.

_____

_____

6. Which volume or volumes would help you find out more about the inventor of the steam locomotive, Richard Trevithick? Explain.

_____

_____

7. Suppose you want to find information about "orphan trains." The library's encyclopedias are 10 years old. Will the information you find be useful to your research? Why or why not?

_____

_____

Directions: Use the almanac table to answer the questions below.

State	Postal Abbreviation	Date Entered Union (United States)
Florida	FL	1845
Georgia	GA	1788
Hawaii	HI	1959
Idaho	ID	1890

8. Using this almanac table, how would you find out if Florida and Georgia were part of the United States in the year 1885?

_____

_____

9. If you wanted to mail a letter to a friend in Atlanta, Georgia, how could this table help you?

_____

_____

10. Why is it important to ask questions about the topic before looking for resources?

_____

_____

Notes for Home: Your child learned about conducting research. *Home Activity:* Name a topic. Have your child ask a question about this topic. Then switch and let your child name the topic. Talk about where you might find answers to your questions.

Compare and Contrast

- To **compare** is to tell how two or more things are alike. To **contrast** is to tell how two or more things are different. Clue words such as *like* or *as* show comparisons. Clue words such as *but* or *unlike* show contrasts.

Directions: Reread Yingtao's descriptions of his two older sisters in "Yingtao's New Friend." Then answer the questions below.

I think Second Sister felt the loneliest. In China, people always said she would turn out to be a real beauty. She had been popular at school there, always surrounded by friends. But in America not many people told her she was beautiful. These days she was often cranky and sad. Mother told the rest of us that we just had to be patient with Second Sister.

Third Sister had no trouble at all making friends. Even before she could speak much English, she began chatting with other kids. She could always fill the gaps with laughter.

From YANG THE YOUNGEST AND HIS TERRIBLE EAR by Lensey Namioka. Copyright © 1992 by Lensey Namioka (Text); Illustrations © by Kees de Kiefte. By permission of Little, Brown and Company.

1. Is Second Sister the same in America as she was in China or is she different? What clue word in the passage tells you?

_____

2. How do you think Second Sister felt in China? Explain.

_____

3. Does Third Sister act like Second Sister? Explain.

_____

4. Write a sentence contrasting the two sisters' behavior in America.

_____

5. Use a separate sheet of paper to tell how you think Yingtao feels in America compared with each of his sisters. Give examples from the story.

Notes for Home: Your child used story details to compare and contrast two characters. *Home Activity:* Work with your child to come up with a list of ways two people he or she knows well are similar (comparisons) and ways they are different (contrasts).

Name_____

1.	Ⓐ	Ⓑ	Ⓒ	Ⓓ
2.	Ⓕ	Ⓖ	Ⓗ	Ⓙ
3.	Ⓐ	Ⓑ	Ⓒ	Ⓓ
4.	Ⓕ	Ⓖ	Ⓗ	Ⓙ
5.	Ⓐ	Ⓑ	Ⓒ	Ⓓ
6.	Ⓕ	Ⓖ	Ⓗ	Ⓙ
7.	Ⓐ	Ⓑ	Ⓒ	Ⓓ
8.	Ⓕ	Ⓖ	Ⓗ	Ⓙ
9.	Ⓐ	Ⓑ	Ⓒ	Ⓓ
10.	Ⓕ	Ⓖ	Ⓗ	Ⓙ
11.	Ⓐ	Ⓑ	Ⓒ	Ⓓ
12.	Ⓕ	Ⓖ	Ⓗ	Ⓙ
13.	Ⓐ	Ⓑ	Ⓒ	Ⓓ
14.	Ⓕ	Ⓖ	Ⓗ	Ⓙ
15.	Ⓐ	Ⓑ	Ⓒ	Ⓓ

Technology: Questions for Inquiry

You can learn about the traditions of another country by **asking questions** and doing research to find answers to your questions. The **Internet** is one place to find answers to your questions. You can use **search engines** to find information. After you type in key words from your questions, the search engine looks for Web sites that may have answers. A search engine home page may look something like this:

Directions: For each topic below, write a question that you could research to find out about life in China.

1. types of food prepared _____

_____

2. games children like to play _____

_____

3. languages spoken _____

_____

_____

Directions: A search engine may give you a list of Web sites that are related to your question or topic. Put an **X** in front of the Web site names listed below that you think may have answers to the question shown on the computer screen.

Where can I find information about holidays celebrated in China?

_____ 4. Folktales from China

_____ 5. Worldwide Holiday Calendar

_____ 6. China Travel and Tourism

_____ 7. Web site of Jamaica

_____ 8. Holidays and Festivals

_____ 9. Chinese Poetry

_____ 10. Holiday Traditions Around the World

Notes for Home: Your child wrote questions and identified possible Web sites that would be useful to find out more about China. *Home Activity:* Play a game in which you give the answer to a question, and your child asks the question that would produce that answer.

Author's Purpose

- An **author's purpose** is the reason or reasons an author has for writing. Four common purposes are to inform, to entertain, to express, and to persuade.
- Often, people read more quickly when the author's purpose is to entertain, and more slowly and carefully when the author has another purpose.

Directions: Reread "Painting Mist and Fog." In the first row of the table, describe the author's purpose or purposes. Use the second row to give supporting reasons to explain why this is the author's purpose. In the last row, tell how quickly or slowly you read the article and why.

Author's Purposes:	1.
Supporting Reasons	2.
Read Quickly or Slowly?	3.

Directions: Think about the author's purpose for these types of writing. Write the purpose of each type in the table.

Comic book	4. Purpose:
How-to instruction book	5. Purpose:

Notes for Home: Your child read a magazine article and identified the author's purpose in writing it. **Home Activity:** Read several different kinds of articles with your child. Have your child figure out the author's purpose for each and give supporting reasons.

Vocabulary

Directions: Choose the word from the box that best completes each sentence. Write the word on the line to the left.

_____ 1. My grandfather makes paintings that are _____ by his childhood.

_____ 2. Once he painted a _____ of children playing ball in a meadow.

_____ 3. Another painting _____ the toys he had when he was little.

_____ 4. From his paintings, I guess that Grandpa has happy _____ of his childhood.

_____ 5. People in the _____ will learn about life long ago from artwork like Grandpa's paintings.

Check the Words You Know
__ border
__ future
__ handkerchief
__ inspired
__ involved
__ laundry
__ memories
__ scene

Directions: Match each word on the left with the word or words on the right that have a similar meaning. Write the letter of the similar word or words on the line.

_____ 6. handkerchief   **a.** washing

_____ 7. border   **b.** included

_____ 8. laundry   **c.** encouraged

_____ 9. inspired   **d.** soft cloth

_____ 10. involved   **e.** boundary

Write a Paragraph

On a separate sheet of paper, write a paragraph about artwork that you saw and liked. It could be a painting in a museum, a picture or photo in your reading book, or even something you made yourself. Tell what you liked and why. Use as many vocabulary words as you can.

Notes for Home: Your child identified and used vocabulary words from *Family Pictures*. *Home Activity:* With your child, look at works of art in a book or magazine. Encourage him or her to talk about the artwork, using as many vocabulary words as possible.

Author's Purpose

- An **author's purpose** is the reason or reasons an author has for writing. Authors often have more than one reason for writing.
- Four common purposes are to inform, to entertain, to express, and to persuade.

1. Reread *Family Pictures*. What do you think is the author's purpose? Write the reason or reasons for writing below. Explain your answer.

_____

_____

Directions: Read each paragraph. Write whether the author's purpose is to inform, entertain, express, or persuade. Explain your answers.

2. The best place to go on vacation is the beach. How can you go wrong with water, sand, and sky? There are people sunning themselves and swimming. There are boats and sand castles. You'll have so much fun.

_____

3. My favorite painting is of the beach. The colors of the water, sand, and sky make me remember all the happy times I had there last summer.

_____

4. Seaweed is any type of plant that grows in the ocean. It can be both a place to live and a source of food for sea creatures.

_____

5. On a separate sheet of paper, write a short paragraph about something that happened to you today. You might inform readers about the day's events, entertain them with a funny story, express how you felt about your day, or try to convince others that it was the best or worst day ever. Below your paragraph, tell your purpose for writing.

Notes for Home: Your child has identified the author's purpose(s) in *Family Pictures* and several short paragraphs. *Home Activity:* Read a short story with your child. Talk about the author's reasons for writing the piece. Was it to inform, entertain, persuade, or express a feeling or mood?

Name_____

1.	Ⓐ	Ⓑ	Ⓒ	Ⓓ
2.	Ⓕ	Ⓖ	Ⓗ	Ⓙ
3.	Ⓐ	Ⓑ	Ⓒ	Ⓓ
4.	Ⓕ	Ⓖ	Ⓗ	Ⓙ
5.	Ⓐ	Ⓑ	Ⓒ	Ⓓ
6.	Ⓕ	Ⓖ	Ⓗ	Ⓙ
7.	Ⓐ	Ⓑ	Ⓒ	Ⓓ
8.	Ⓕ	Ⓖ	Ⓗ	Ⓙ
9.	Ⓐ	Ⓑ	Ⓒ	Ⓓ
10.	Ⓕ	Ⓖ	Ⓗ	Ⓙ
11.	Ⓐ	Ⓑ	Ⓒ	Ⓓ
12.	Ⓕ	Ⓖ	Ⓗ	Ⓙ
13.	Ⓐ	Ⓑ	Ⓒ	Ⓓ
14.	Ⓕ	Ⓖ	Ⓗ	Ⓙ
15.	Ⓐ	Ⓑ	Ⓒ	Ⓓ

Selection Test

Directions: Choose the best answer to each item. Mark the letter for the answer you have chosen.

Part 1: Vocabulary

Find the answer choice that means about the same as the underlined word in each sentence.

1. Anna plans for the <u>future</u>.
   A. special friend
   B. favorite hobby
   C. problem or worry
   D. time to come

2. Tell us what is happening in this <u>scene</u>.
   F. time of year; season
   G. place of work
   H. a view or picture
   J. faraway land

3. The <u>border</u> is 100 miles from here.
   A. nearest neighbor
   B. boundary of a country or state
   C. grandparent's house
   D. woods or forest

4. I bought a yellow <u>handkerchief</u>.
   F. square cloth for wiping the nose
   G. colorful flag or banner
   H. pair of gloves
   J. large woolen blanket

5. Enrique shared some of his childhood <u>memories</u>.
   A. old toys
   B. things that a person remembers
   C. songs that tell a story
   D. drawings or paintings

6. Grandpa <u>inspired</u> me to write a poem.
   F. allowed
   G. ordered
   H. gave confidence to
   J. taught how

7. Please put the <u>laundry</u> away.
   A. dress-up clothes
   B. rags used for cleaning
   C. fabric to be cut and sewn
   D. clothes that have been washed

8. The girls are <u>involved</u> in their chores.
   F. proud of
   G. busy or occupied
   H. tired of
   J. skilled at

GO ON

Part 2: Comprehension

Use what you know about the selection to answer each item.

9. What did the author dream of being when she grew up?
   A. a poet
   B. an artist
   C. an actress
   D. a mother

10. What did the author do at her grandmother's house?
   F. hung laundry
   G. caught a shark
   H. picked oranges
   J. made tamales

11. Which step comes last when preparing a meal of nopal cactus?
   A. shaving off the needles
   B. boiling in hot water
   C. cutting into pieces
   D. frying with chili powder and eggs

12. Which of these was a frightening experience for the author?
   F. hitting a piñata
   G. seeing a hammerhead shark
   H. being up on the roof
   J. picking nopal cactus

13. The author probably included the part called "Beds for Dreaming" to—
   A. tell about a funny event.
   B. explain what her house was like.
   C. describe a holiday custom.
   D. express important feelings she had as a girl.

14. One of the author's main purposes for writing this selection was to—
   F. compare her family with other families.
   G. share special times she had with her family.
   H. tell how people in a family should behave.
   J. describe each member of her family.

15. Who does the author feel most grateful to for helping her make her dreams come true?
   A. her father
   B. her grandparents
   C. her sister
   D. her mother

STOP

Fact and Opinion

Directions: Read the story. Then read each question about the story. Choose the best answer to each question. Mark the letter for the answer you have chosen.

A Visit to the Museum

My class went to the art museum last month. I thought I would be bored, but I was in for a big surprise. We saw paintings by the artist Van Gogh. But his flowers were beautiful. One of the paintings was of a sunny field. In the art world, it is called a *landscape*.

We had pizza for lunch, which was OK. Then we saw paintings of laundry. I pass laundry every day, but I never look at it. I guess going to a museum can get a person to see things differently.

1. Which is a story fact?
   A. The class went to the museum.
   B. The narrator decided to become a painter.
   C. Van Gogh is a cool artist.
   D. The class went by bus.

2. Which sentence contains both fact and opinion?
   F. I thought I would be bored.
   G. Then we saw paintings of laundry.
   H. In the art world, it is called a *landscape*.
   J. We had pizza for lunch, which was OK.

3. Which sentence from this story states an opinion?
   A. I pass laundry every day, but I never look at it.
   B. I guess going to a museum can get a person to see things differently.
   C. We saw paintings by the artist Van Gogh.
   D. In the art world, it is called a *landscape*.

4. Which sentence states a fact about Van Gogh?
   F. Van Gogh made strange-looking sculptures.
   G. Van Gogh's paintings are boring.
   H. Van Gogh's flowers are cool.
   J. Van Gogh painted flowers and landscapes.

5. Which word or words in the last sentence are a clue that the sentence is an opinion?
   A. can
   B. differently
   C. museum
   D. I guess

Notes for Home: Your child has read a story and used story details to tell fact from opinion. *Home Activity:* Take turns with your child making statements that are either fact or opinion. Identify the type of statement the other person makes.

Phonics: Common Word Patterns

Directions: Read each word below. Some words have a word pattern as in **home**: consonant-vowel-consonant-e. Other words have a word pattern as in **basket**: vowel-consonant-consonant-vowel. Write each word in the correct column.

rope	cactus	tale	same	summer	tender
brother	time	shelter	line	sister	make

CVCe
home

1. _____
2. _____
3. _____
4. _____
5. _____
6. _____

VCCV
basket

7. _____
8. _____
9. _____
10. _____
11. _____
12. _____

Directions: Read each sentence. Find an example of each word pattern (**CVCe, VCCV**) in each sentence. Write the words in the correct columns.

CVCe   VCCV

_____ _____ **13.** Our summer at the beach was fine.

_____ _____ **14.** My mother made cookies.

_____ _____ **15.** My sister hung a rope from a tree for a bird feeder.

_____ _____ **16.** Birds came to the feeder and took shelter in a nearby tree.

_____ _____ **17.** My aunt gave us oranges for lunch.

_____ _____ **18.** We played a funny game later.

_____ _____ **19.** Then my brother said we had to go home.

_____ _____ **20.** It was after nine when we left.

Notes for Home: Your child learned to recognize two common word patterns: *CVCe (home)* and *VCCV (basket)*. **Home Activity:** Say each word in the box. Have your child listen for the long vowel sounds in *CVCe* and the short vowel sounds in the first syllable of *VCCV* words.

Outline

Making an **outline** can help you organize information you read. Outlining helps you remember important points and understand what you read. Outlining information can also help you prepare for tests.

Directions: Read this article about flowers found in Texas. Then use the information in this article to complete the outline on the next page.

Texas *Wildflowers*

by William G. Morales

Mexican Hat

Texas Dandelion

Indian Paintbrush

Many people know the old folk song, "The Yellow Rose of Texas." Texas is home to many beautiful wildflowers too.

If you see a yellow-orange flower that looks like a sombrero, you probably have found a flower called a **Mexican Hat.** These pretty flowers are also called "coneflowers" and "thimbleflowers." Mexican Hat flowers can be used for making dye.

Another flower found in the Lone Star State is the **Texas Dandelion.** These members of the sunflower family are found in pastures, near roads, and on people's lawns. When the stems of these flowers are broken, they leak a kind of milky sap. When the seeds dry, children enjoy blowing them into the air.

One of the most beautiful flowers in Texas is the **Indian Paintbrush,** also known as "the scarlet paintbrush." The paintbrush plants use the roots of other plants to help them grow. They bloom from March to May, but are the prettiest in April.

12

Texas Wildflowers

I. _____

    A.   Also called coneflowers and _____

    B.   Used for making dye

II. _____

    A.   When broken, they leak milky sap.

    B.   Found near pastures, roads, and on _____

    C.   Children blow the seeds in the air.

III. Indian Paintbrush

    A.   Also known as _____

    B.   Uses the roots of other plants to grow

Directions: Explain why an outline can be useful for researching and studying. Write your explanation on the lines below.

_____

_____

_____

_____

_____

_____

_____

_____

Notes for Home: Your child used an outline to organize information and understand what he or she read. **Home Activity:** Create an outline that organizes information about an interesting topic, such as your family history or wildlife in your area. Use the above outline as a model.

Character

- **Characters** are the people or animals in a story or nonfictional article.
- You can learn about characters by what they think, do, and say.
- You can also learn about characters by seeing how other characters in the story treat them and what other characters say about them.

Directions: Reread "Ma on the Prairie." Fill in the word web with story details about Ma that help you learn about her. On the line at the bottom of the page, write your own description of this character.

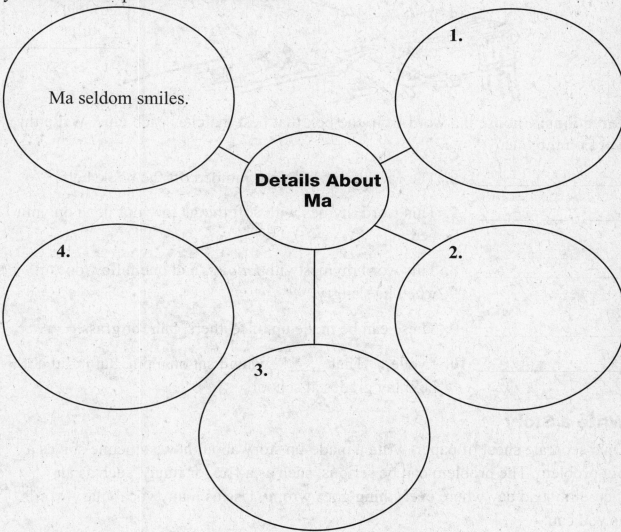

Ma seldom smiles.

1.

Details About Ma

4.

2.

3.

5. My description of Ma: _____

Notes for Home: Your child read a story and identified details that helped her or him understand a main character. ***Home Activity:*** Have your child try to understand a person better by making a list of things that person does and says and what other people say about the person.

Vocabulary

Directions: Draw a line to connect each word on the left with its definition on the right.

1. tufts   roars
2. smarted   stooped
3. bellows   clumps of grass
4. crouched   waves of smoke
5. billows   stung

Directions: Choose the word from the box that best matches each clue. Write the word on the line.

_____ 6. The cat did this before it jumped off the bookshelf.

_____ 7. This word rhymes with soft things for your head on your bed.

_____ 8. This word rhymes with *fellows,* and one fellow does it when he's angry.

_____ 9. These can be made up of feathers, hair, or grass.

_____ 10. I yelled, "That ____!" when I sat on a pin, but it did not help my grades at school.

Write a Story

On a separate sheet of paper, write a made-up story about how someone solves a big problem. The problem can be serious, such as a fire, or funny, such as an incredibly bad day where everything goes wrong. Use as many vocabulary words as you can.

Notes for Home: Your child identified and used vocabulary words from "Addie in Charge." *Home Activity:* Say the vocabulary word *crouched* and have your child act out its meaning. Take turns saying other action words that can be acted out by the other person.

Name_____

Character

- **Characters** are the people or animals in a story.
- You can learn about characters by what they think, do, and say. You can also learn about characters by how other characters in the story treat them and what other characters say about them.

Directions: Reread what happens in "Addie in Charge" when she tries to save herself and her little brother from the fire. Then answer the questions below. Think about how you learn what Addie and Burt are like.

> Still kneeling on the ground, Addie used one foot to carefully feel for the ladder's highest rung. Slowly, she lowered herself, balancing Burt with great effort. Down into the well she went, step over step. Now they were below ground level. It was pitch black, and the water felt cold around Addie's knees as she reached the bottom rung. "Don't let go, Burt. Don't let go," she told her brother, who buried his face into the back of her neck so that her necklace dug deep into her skin.
>
> From ADDIE ACROSS THE PRAIRIE by Laurie Lawlor. Text copyright ©1986 by Laurie Lawlor. Excerpt reprinted by permission of Albert Whitman & Company.

1. Is Addie sure of herself? How do you know?

_____

2. How do you know Addie cares about her brother?

_____

3. How do you think Burt feels? How do you know?

_____

4. Addie's parents left her in charge. How do you think they felt about her?

_____

5. On a separate sheet of paper, describe Addie in your own words. Use details from the story to support your answers.

Notes for Home: Your child has read a story and used story details to understand characters. **Home Activity:** Help your child understand characters in books you read together by talking about the things they think, do, or say.

Name_____

1.	Ⓐ	Ⓑ	Ⓒ	Ⓓ
2.	Ⓕ	Ⓖ	Ⓗ	Ⓙ
3.	Ⓐ	Ⓑ	Ⓒ	Ⓓ
4.	Ⓕ	Ⓖ	Ⓗ	Ⓙ
5.	Ⓐ	Ⓑ	Ⓒ	Ⓓ
6.	Ⓕ	Ⓖ	Ⓗ	Ⓙ
7.	Ⓐ	Ⓑ	Ⓒ	Ⓓ
8.	Ⓕ	Ⓖ	Ⓗ	Ⓙ
9.	Ⓐ	Ⓑ	Ⓒ	Ⓓ
10.	Ⓕ	Ⓖ	Ⓗ	Ⓙ
11.	Ⓐ	Ⓑ	Ⓒ	Ⓓ
12.	Ⓕ	Ⓖ	Ⓗ	Ⓙ
13.	Ⓐ	Ⓑ	Ⓒ	Ⓓ
14.	Ⓕ	Ⓖ	Ⓗ	Ⓙ
15.	Ⓐ	Ⓑ	Ⓒ	Ⓓ

Selection Test

Directions: Choose the best answer to each item. Mark the letter for the answer you have chosen.

Part 1: Vocabulary

Find the answer choice that means about the same as the underlined word in each sentence.

1. Stella crouched on the floor.
   A. spun around quickly
   B. stooped low with bent legs
   C. walked on tiptoes
   D. pounded with the feet

2. I could hear the cow's bellows.
   F. deep breaths
   G. rings from a bell
   H. sweet songs
   J. loud, deep noises

3. Grains of sand smarted my face.
   A. caused pain in
   B. stuck to
   C. blew around
   D. covered

4. We pulled tufts of weeds from the garden.
   F. seeds
   G. roots
   H. bunches
   J. flowers

5. Billows of smoke rose from the roof.
   A. thin streams
   B. large piles
   C. great waves
   D. storm clouds

Part 2: Comprehension

Use what you know about the story to answer each item.

6. When the story begins, Addie's parents and brother were—
   F. traveling to Iowa.
   G. planting crops.
   H. visiting neighbors.
   J. building a sod home.

7. Who was Ruby Lillian?
   A. Addie's friend from Iowa
   B. the Fencys' cow
   C. Addie's little sister
   D. a doll

8. What clue shows that Addie was quite grown-up and dependable?
   F. She was left in charge of her little brother for two days.
   G. She was making a sampler.
   H. She saw a strange light in the sky.
   J. She read Burt a story.

GO ON

9. What was the first sign of trouble that Addie noticed?
   A. The horizon was orange and yellow.
   B. Coyotes ran through the field.
   C. The cows were making frightened noises.
   D. Ashes were flying in the air.

10. As the fire drew closer, Addie felt—
   F. sure the firebreak would stop the fire.
   G. terrified but determined to stay safe.
   H. sure that she and Burt were going to die.
   J. nervous but certain that her parents would rescue her.

11. Why did Addie climb down into the well?
   A. She knew fire could not go there.
   B. It was quiet and dark.
   C. She and Burt needed water to drink.
   D. It was far from the fire's path.

12. In the well, Addie felt—
   F. too afraid to do anything.
   G. afraid, but responsible for her brother's safety.
   H. in control of the situation.
   J. angry that her parents had left her alone.

13. When George found a scrap of Addie's bonnet, he thought that Addie and Burt had—
   A. hidden in the well.
   B. run away from the fire.
   C. hidden in the root cellar.
   D. died in the fire.

14. For Addie, what was the best thing to come out of her experience?
   F. She would never quarrel with George again.
   G. She discovered that she was strong enough to be a pioneer.
   H. Her parents probably wouldn't leave her alone again.
   J. The Fencys would always be grateful to her.

15. What was the most important thing Addie did in this story?
   A. threw water on the Fencys' house
   B. put Anna Fency's trunk in the cellar
   C. kept herself and her brother safe
   D. untied Bess and Missy

STOP

Theme

Directions: Read the story. Then read each question about the story. Choose the best answer to each question. Mark the letter for the answer you have chosen.

Helping Hans

Ten-year-old Hans and his father were building a table. Hans was proud to be helping his father. Anna, his little sister, wanted to help too, but Hans said, "Go play with your dolls. You're too little to help."

When Hans and his father finished sawing, they began to put the table together. They pounded nail after nail. At last, just one leg was left, but there were no more nails.

Hans and his father searched everywhere, but they could not find any nails. Little Anna, playing quietly on the floor, suddenly pounced.

"Here they are!" she said. The nails had rolled across the floor to where she was playing.

"Thank you, Anna," said Hans. "You're a big help!"

1. A story's theme is—
   A. what happens.
   B. its big idea.
   C. its ending.
   D. why something happens.

2. Which statement best describes this story's theme?
   F. Don't build anything unless you have all the pieces.
   G. Even the littlest can help.
   H. Don't drop the nails before the table is finished.
   J. Children should be seen but not heard.

3. The theme of this passage is—
   A. stated by Hans.
   B. stated by Hans's father.
   C. stated by Anna.
   D. Not stated directly by any one character.

4. A title that suggests the theme is—
   F. Little Helpers.
   G. We Need Nails.
   H. Stop! Look! Listen!
   J. Table Building Long Ago.

5. Which statement from the story supports the theme?
   A. There were no more nails.
   B. They pounded nail after nail.
   C. "You're a big help!"
   D. Ten-year-old Hans and his father were building a table.

Notes for Home: Your child has read a story and used story details to identify its theme. *Home Activity:* When you and your child are watching television together, suggest that he or she tell the theme of a story and give reasons to support his or her answer.

Phonics: Three-letter Blends

Directions: Read each short word. Make a longer word by following the first instruction. Take that longer word and make an even longer word by following the second instruction. Write each new word on the line.

1. sash

Add an **l** after the first **s.** _____

Add a **p** after the first **s.** _____

2. tee

Add an **r** after the **t.** _____

Add an **h** after the **t.** _____

3. ream

Add a **c** before the **r.** _____

Add an **s** before the **c.** _____

4. sing

Add a **t** after the **s.** _____

Add an **r** after the **t.** _____

Directions: The sentences below are part of a diary entry about solving a problem. Six words start with a three-letter blend. Write the six words on the lines.

Dear Diary,

When Sandy and I were hiking, we came to a stream. We tested how deep the water was by throwing some rocks in it. Since it was pretty shallow, we took off our shoes and waded through the water. We were afraid we were lost in the woods, but then we heard cars. We squinted our eyes to see better, and Sandy screamed, "Look, there's the street!"

5. _____

6. _____

7. _____

8. _____

9. _____

10. _____

Notes for Home: Your child learned words such as *splash* that start with three-letter blend. *Home Activity:* Read labels with your child to help identify other three-letter blends, such as those that begin *str-, spl-, scr-, spr-, squ-,* or *thr-*. List the words you find.

Parts of a Book

Knowing the **parts of a book** makes it easier to locate information. For example, a **table of contents** shows what a book is about and where to find each chapter.

Directions: Use the table of contents to answer the questions that follow.

1. What do the numbers shown on the right of the table of contents tell you?

_____

2. How do the topics under each chapter head help you? _____

_____

_____

3. How many different people can you read about in Chapter 2? _____

4. If you wanted to research American Pioneers who were women, which chapter should you read? On what page does this chapter begin?

_____

5. Which chapter should you read to learn more about Buffalo Bill?

_____

An **index** is a list of the specific subjects covered in a book. It tells what pages have information about each subject.

Directions: Study this index from *American Pioneers of the Wild West*. Use it to answer the questions that follow.

Index

Americans, Native, 40, 51–65
  customs of, 40
  folk tales of, 60–65
  speeches, 51–59
Bill, Buffalo, 11–13
Buffaloes, 35–39
  herding of, 38
  near extinction, 36–37

Carson, Kit, 25–27
Cowboys (General), 8, 80–104
  daily life of, 101–104
  dude ranches, 81
  horse training, 98
  meals of, 8
  museums, 83

---

6. If you wanted to find information about a famous Native American speech, which pages would you read?

_____

7. If you wanted to know what cowboys ate for dinner, which page would you read?

_____

8. If you wanted to use an index to find information about a person, would you look under the first name or last name?

_____

9. If you looked on pages 25–27, what information would you expect to find?

_____

10. How does a table of contents and an index help you find information quickly?

_____

_____

Notes for Home: Your child learned about the parts of a book, such as the table of contents and the index. *Home Activity:* Challenge your child to locate information in a nonfiction book, using the index and table of contents.

Name _____

Visualizing

- To **visualize** means to form a picture in your mind as you read.
- As you read, look for details that tell how things look, smell, sound, taste, and feel.

Directions: Reread "Caught in the Kitchen." Then complete the web. Write details from the story that help you picture the characters and setting.

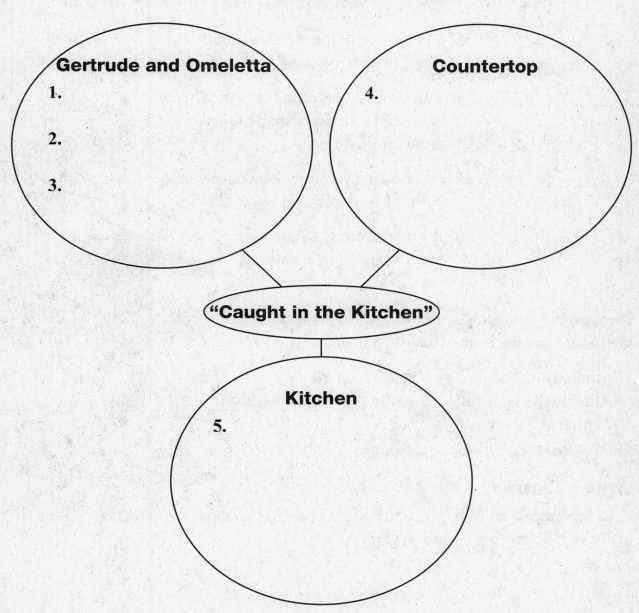

Gertrude and Omeletta
1.

2.

3.

Countertop
4.

"Caught in the Kitchen"

Kitchen
5.

Notes for Home: Your child pictured events and characters in his or her mind while reading. *Home Activity:* Ask your child to visualize a favorite place. Invite him or her to tell you sights, smells, sounds, tastes, and sensations associated with that place.

Vocabulary

Directions: Choose the word from the box that best completes each sentence. Write the word on the line to the left.

_____ **1.** It is always a special _____ when my family goes to the city.

_____ **2.** We take the train into the city because the _____ station is close by.

_____ **3.** Once we're in the city, we usually travel by underground _____.

_____ **4.** Traveling underground gets us where we want to go faster than trying to drive through heavy _____.

_____ **5.** Once, when we were at a concert in the park, I heard a cricket _____.

_____ **6.** It wasn't exactly singing a _____, but it sounded nice anyway.

Directions: Circle the word that has the same or nearly the same meaning as the first word in each group.

7. melody	words	tune	ringing
8. furiously	wildly	softly	lightly
9. chirp	bark	tweet	growl
10. venturing	frying	risking	staying

Write a Letter

On a separate sheet of paper, write a letter to a friend about a trip to a city. Use as many vocabulary words as you can.

Notes for Home: Your child identified and used new vocabulary from *The Cricket in Times Square*. **Home Activity:** With your child, make a list of imaginary, fun trips and describe how you would travel. Use the vocabulary words, such as *railroad* or *subway,* in your planning.

Visualizing

- **Visualizing** means creating a picture or pictures in your mind as you read.
- If you have trouble visualizing, you may want to reread parts of the story.

Directions: Reread about Tucker Mouse in *The Cricket in Times Square*. Then answer the questions below. Think about what it says in the story to help you visualize.

Tucker Mouse had been watching the Bellinis and listening to what they said. Next to scrounging, eavesdropping on human beings was what he enjoyed most. That was one of the reasons he lived in the Times Square subway station. As soon as the family disappeared, he darted out across the floor and scooted up to the newsstand. At one side the boards had separated and there was a wide space he could jump through. He'd been in a few times before—just exploring. For a moment he stood under the three legged stool, letting his eyes get used to the darkness. Then he jumped up on it.

Excerpt from "Chester" from THE CRICKET IN TIMES SQUARE by George Selden, pictures by Garth Williams. Copyright ©1960 by George Selden Thompson and Garth Williams. Copyright renewed © 1988 by George Selden Thompson.   Reprinted by permission of Farrar, Straus & Giroux, Inc.

1. Where is Tucker at the very beginning of the passage? How do you know?

_____

2. Where does Tucker go when the family leaves? Is he moving quickly or slowly?

_____

3. How does Tucker get into the newsstand? Is it difficult or easy? Explain.

_____

4. Is it easy or hard for Tucker to see? How do you know?

_____

5. Pick another scene from the story. On a separate sheet of paper, tell what mental pictures you have as you read. Give examples of words or details that help you visualize the scene.

Notes for Home: Your child has read a story and used story details to visualize it by creating a mental picture of the story. *Home Activity:* With your child, look at a descriptive passage in a favorite book or story. Invite your child to tell you what he or she imagines while reading.

Name_____

1.	Ⓐ	Ⓑ	Ⓒ	Ⓓ
2.	Ⓕ	Ⓖ	Ⓗ	Ⓙ
3.	Ⓐ	Ⓑ	Ⓒ	Ⓓ
4.	Ⓕ	Ⓖ	Ⓗ	Ⓙ
5.	Ⓐ	Ⓑ	Ⓒ	Ⓓ
6.	Ⓕ	Ⓖ	Ⓗ	Ⓙ
7.	Ⓐ	Ⓑ	Ⓒ	Ⓓ
8.	Ⓕ	Ⓖ	Ⓗ	Ⓙ
9.	Ⓐ	Ⓑ	Ⓒ	Ⓓ
10.	Ⓕ	Ⓖ	Ⓗ	Ⓙ
11.	Ⓐ	Ⓑ	Ⓒ	Ⓓ
12.	Ⓕ	Ⓖ	Ⓗ	Ⓙ
13.	Ⓐ	Ⓑ	Ⓒ	Ⓓ
14.	Ⓕ	Ⓖ	Ⓗ	Ⓙ
15.	Ⓐ	Ⓑ	Ⓒ	Ⓓ

Selection Test

Directions: Choose the best answer to each item. Mark the letter for the answer you have chosen.

Part 1: Vocabulary

Find the answer choice that means about the same as the underlined word in each sentence.

1. The boys worked <u>furiously</u>.
   - A.   without much interest
   - B.   in a slow, careful way
   - C.   quickly and wildly
   - D.   in a cheerful way

2. The <u>chirp</u> came from inside that box.
   - F.   short sharp sound
   - G.   beat of a drum
   - H.   loud flapping sound
   - J.   low moan

3. The children were <u>venturing</u> into the woods.
   - A.   shouting or calling
   - B.   daring to go
   - C.   hiking fast
   - D.   staring

4. I have heard that <u>melody</u> before.
   - F.   idea
   - G.   joke or funny story
   - H.   tune
   - J.   signal or message

5. Everyone was there for the <u>occasion</u>.
   - A.   talk or discussion
   - B.   special event
   - C.   lesson or class
   - D.   small meal

6. We met at the <u>railroad</u> station.
   - F.   taxi
   - G.   police
   - H.   bus
   - J.   train

7. Watch out for the <u>traffic</u>.
   - A.   cars and buses moving along streets
   - B.   rules of safe driving
   - C.   signs for drivers on highways
   - D.   rest stop for travelers

8. We decided to take the <u>subway</u>.
   - F.   ship that travels under water
   - G.   bridge over a city street
   - H.   underground electric train
   - J.   train that travels at night

GO ON

Part 2: Comprehension

Use what you know about the story to answer each item.

9. At the beginning of the story, Tucker Mouse is in a—
   A. subway station.
   B. tree stump.
   C. bus station.
   D. city apartment.

10. What did Tucker Mouse give Chester to eat?
    F. roast beef
    G. liverwurst
    H. eggs
    J. chocolate

11. At the beginning of the story, how did Chester feel about being in New York?
    A. excited and amazed
    B. bored and sleepy
    C. surprised and glad
    D. nervous and uncomfortable

12. Which words match your mental picture of Chester's journey inside the picnic basket?
    F. dark and cramped
    G. quiet and smooth
    H. cozy and comfortable
    J. smelly and dirty

13. Which detail from the story helps create a mental picture of New York City at night?
    A. "And there he gasped, holding his breath and crouching against the cement."
    B. "They were standing at one corner of the Times building."
    C. "Above the cricket, towers that seemed like mountains of light rose up into the night sky."
    D. "'Well—it's—it's quite something,' Chester stuttered."

14. What was the luckiest thing that Chester did in this story?
    F. hopping into a picnic basket
    G. riding in a subway
    H. meeting Tucker Mouse
    J. climbing up the pipe

15. At the end of the story, Chester has probably decided to—
    A. move to New York for good.
    B. find a way to escape from Tucker Mouse and Harry Cat.
    C. return to Connecticut right away.
    D. let his new friends show him New York for a little while.

STOP

Making Judgments

Directions: Read the story. Then read each question about the story. Choose the best answer to each question. Mark the letter for the answer you have chosen.

The Best Place to Live

Maria lives in the big city of Chicago. Jade lives in a little town called Gladstone. Maria says that Chicago is the best place to live in the whole world. Jade says that nobody should live in a big city because small towns are best!

When Maria went to visit Jade, Jade invited all her friends to meet Maria.

When Jade visited Maria, Maria took her to the top of Chicago's tallest building. Jade felt scared being so high up, so they went down right away. Then Jade started to have a good time. She began to think that big cities might be just as nice as small towns.

Maria wants to bring Jade back to the tall building again. She hopes they go there before it's time for Jade to leave.

1. A word that describes how Maria and Jade feel about where they live is—
   A. embarrassed.
   B. proud.
   C. bored.
   D. afraid.

2. When Jade invited all her friends to meet Maria, she was probably trying to make Maria feel—
   F. lonely.
   G. welcome.
   H. confused.
   J. angry.

3. When Maria took Jade to the top of Chicago's tallest building, she probably wanted Jade to feel—
   A. scared.
   B. sick.
   C. excited.
   D. angry.

4. Jade changed her mind about big cities because she was—
   F. lonely.
   G. wishy-washy.
   H. confused.
   J. open-minded.

5. Maria wants Jade to go back to the building so that Jade will—
   A. feel scared again.
   B. like being at the top.
   C. get sick.
   D. like Maria more.

Notes for Home: Your child made judgments about characters in a short story. *Home Activity:* Invite your child to share times when someone was a good friend and when someone was not a good friend.

Phonics: Diphthongs

Directions: Read the words in the box. Say the words to yourself. Listen to the vowel sounds. Some words have the vowel sound in **found.** Other words have the vowel sound in **boy.** Write each word in the correct column.

scrounge	enjoyed	down	pointed	about
house	voice	noise	town	boiled

found

1. _____

2. _____

3. _____

4. _____

5. _____

boy

6. _____

7. _____

8. _____

9. _____

10. _____

Directions: Read each sentence. Say the underlined word to yourself. Then read the words in ( ). Circle the word that has the same vowel sound as the underlined word.

11. New York City is a big <u>town</u>. (house/voice)

12. The cars and people make a lot of <u>noise</u>. (down/boy)

13. You have to walk <u>down</u> some stairs to get to the

    subway. (mouse/enjoyed)

14. Riding a bus is an easy way to get <u>around</u> in a

    big city. (about/boiled)

15. If you visit New York City, you will <u>enjoy</u> walking

    along Fifth Avenue. (town/noise)

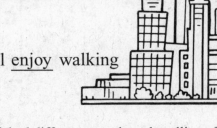

Notes for Home: Your child distinguished different sounds and spellings for the vowel sounds in *town* and *noise*. **Home Activity:** Help your child list words with *oi* and *oy* that stand for the vowel sound in *noise* and with *ou* and *ow* that stand for the vowel sound in *town*.

© Scott Foresman 4

Newspapers/Magazines/Periodicals

Newspapers are published daily or weekly and contain news, advertisements, feature stories, editorials, and other useful, current information.

Directions: Read the front page headlines of these newspapers. Use the information to answer the questions that follow.

1. Would you expect to find an article on how to make and use skateboards in the *New York City Business News Today?* Explain.

   _____

   _____

2. Is the headline for *The New York City Daily Reporter* the beginning of a news story, an editorial, or an advertisement?

   _____

3. A well-known actor is coming to New York City to film a movie. Which paper is most likely to cover this story?

   _____

4. Why are newspapers helpful sources of information? _____

   _____

5. Would you use last week's newspaper to find out about the original construction of Times Square? Explain.

   _____

   _____

Name _____

Magazines, also called **periodicals,** are published at set intervals (weekly, monthly, quarterly, and so on). They may contain news articles, opinion columns, advertisements, cartoons, reports, and other current information. They often focus on a particular subject. The name of the magazine will usually tell you what subject is covered.

Directions: Use information from the magazine covers here to answer the questions that follow.

6. Which magazine might have useful information about baseball?

_____

7. Will you find stories about snakes in *Dogs & Cats?* Explain. _____

_____

8. Which magazine will tell you about theater shows?

_____

9. If you are doing a report on nutrition and want to find some healthful snacks to suggest, what magazine might have an article of interest?

_____

10. If you needed to find out about a concert that took place in Central Park yesterday, would you look in a newspaper or a magazine? Explain.

_____

_____

 Notes for Home: Your child learned about using newspapers and magazines as resources. *Home Activity:* Look at newspapers and magazines together. What does the name of the publication tell you? Use headlines or a table of contents to scan for articles of interest.

Name _____

Cause and Effect

- A **cause** is why something happened. An **effect** is what happened.
- Sometimes a cause can have more than one effect.
- Sometimes there are clue words like *because, so, if, then,* or *since* to help you figure out what happened and why.

Cause	Effect
Cause	**Effect**

Directions: Reread "Super Cooper Scoopers." Then complete the table. Write the effect or effects for each cause given.

Cause (Why did it happen?)	Effect (What happened?)
Because the creek was dirty,	1.
	2.
	3.
Because garbage gets ripped apart in creeks and spreads,	4.
Because the creek is now clean,	5.

Notes for Home: Your child read a news article and explained the effects of events. *Home Activity:* Talk about a recent happy family event, such as a pleasant dinner together or a special trip. Help your child identify the reasons that caused the event to be so enjoyable.

Vocabulary

Directions: Choose the word from the box that best completes each sentence. Write the word on the line to the left.

_____ 1. The garden _____ arrived in the mail yesterday.

_____ 2. We were _____ by how many seeds and plants it showed.

_____ 3. When we shovel dirt in the garden, we'll wear gloves so we don't get _____ on our hands.

_____ 4. We will _____ our beautiful garden by having a garden party when we're done.

_____ 5. We will have to remember to put a _____ on the gate to keep our dogs out of the garden.

Directions: Choose the word from the box that best matches each clue. Write the letters of the word on the blanks. The boxed letters spell something found near a garden.

6. illustrated list   6. ___ ___ ___ ___ ___ □ ___ ___

7. have a party   7. ___ ___ ___ ___ ___ □ ___ ___ ___

8. lock you can remove   8. ___ □ ___ ___ ___ ___ ___ ___

9. sores on your skin   9. ___ ___ ___ □ ___ ___ ___ ___

10. influenced deeply   10. ___ ___ ___ ___ □ ___ ___ ___ ___

Something found near a garden: ___ ___ ___ ___ ___

Write Instructions

On a separate sheet of paper, give instructions for growing flowers or vegetables. Use as many of the vocabulary words as you can.

Notes for Home: Your child identified and used vocabulary words from "A Big-City Dream."
Home Activity: Create a picture catalog with your child. It can show flowers, vegetables, or any items that your child can identify. Write a caption for each picture drawn.

Cause and Effect

- A **cause** is why something happens. An **effect** is what happens.
- A cause may have more than one effect. An effect may have more than one cause.
- Sometimes a clue word such as *because* or *since* signals a cause-effect relationship. Sometimes there is no clue word.

Directions: Reread what happens in "A Big-City Dream" when Rosie appears. Then answer the questions below. Think about what it says in the story to help you identify causes and effects.

> Lots of people walk past. Most of them don't even notice what we're doing. And nobody offers to help.
>
> Then, all of the sudden, I see Rosie and her mom turn the corner. My heart rises straight up in my chest.
>
> Yay! I want to shout. You're coming after all!
>
> I wipe my sweaty face on my sleeves. I get ready to run over and open the gate extra wide to let her in. But Rosie doesn't even look at me. My heart falls down, hard, when she walks right past without even turning her head.
>
> . From WEST SIDE KIDS: THE BIG IDEA by Ellen Schecter. Text copyright © 1996 by Bank Street College of Education. Reprinted with permission of Hyperion Books for Children.

1. What causes the narrator's heart to rise "straight up in her chest"?

_____

2. Why does the narrator want to shout "Yay! You're coming after all!"

_____

3. Why do you think Rosie walks right past "without even turning her head"?

_____

4. How does the narrator feel when Rosie walks past her? How do you know?

_____

5. On a separate sheet of paper, tell two things that cause the narrator to feel happy and two things that cause her to feel sad.

Notes for Home: Your child has read a story and used story details to understand cause and effect. **Home Activity:** Play a cause and effect game with your child. You name a cause *(It started to rain.)* and invite your child to name an effect *(We got our umbrellas.).*

1.	Ⓐ	Ⓑ	Ⓒ	Ⓓ
2.	Ⓕ	Ⓖ	Ⓗ	Ⓙ
3.	Ⓐ	Ⓑ	Ⓒ	Ⓓ
4.	Ⓕ	Ⓖ	Ⓗ	Ⓙ
5.	Ⓐ	Ⓑ	Ⓒ	Ⓓ
6.	Ⓕ	Ⓖ	Ⓗ	Ⓙ
7.	Ⓐ	Ⓑ	Ⓒ	Ⓓ
8.	Ⓕ	Ⓖ	Ⓗ	Ⓙ
9.	Ⓐ	Ⓑ	Ⓒ	Ⓓ
10.	Ⓕ	Ⓖ	Ⓗ	Ⓙ
11.	Ⓐ	Ⓑ	Ⓒ	Ⓓ
12.	Ⓕ	Ⓖ	Ⓗ	Ⓙ
13.	Ⓐ	Ⓑ	Ⓒ	Ⓓ
14.	Ⓕ	Ⓖ	Ⓗ	Ⓙ
15.	Ⓐ	Ⓑ	Ⓒ	Ⓓ

Selection Test

Directions: Choose the best answer to each item. Mark the letter for the answer you have chosen.

Part 1: Vocabulary

Find the answer choice that means the same as the underlined word in each sentence.

1. We will need a padlock.
   A. area enclosed with a fence
   B. gardening tool
   C. lock that can be put on and removed
   D. set of keys

2. I noticed Nell's blisters.
   F. sores on the skin
   G. small bandages
   H. rips or tears in clothing
   J. deep wrinkles

3. Mike looked at the catalog.
   A. finished project
   B. list of jobs to be done
   C. people working together
   D. book of things for sale

4. The teacher was impressed.
   F. strongly affected
   G. treated in a mean way
   H. remembered with fondness
   J. entertained or amused

5. The parents and children will celebrate together.
   A. solve a problem by talking
   B. have activities for a special day
   C. share work equally
   D. learn new skills

Part 2: Comprehension

Use what you know about the story to answer each item.

6. On Saturday morning, Luz hurried to meet—
   F. Ms. Kline.
   G. Papi.
   H. Rosie.
   J. Mami.

7. When Luz got to the corner on the first day, the first thing she looked for was—
   A. Rosie.
   B. the Green Giant.
   C. the red tulip.
   D. a rake.

8. Rosie probably did not help Luz because—
   F. she was too busy.
   G. her mother would not let her.
   H. she was upset with Luz.
   J. she didn't have work clothes.

GO ON

9. Luz worked without complaining
   because she—
   A. was so happy with the way the
      lot looked.
   B. needed the exercise.
   C. did not want to be scolded.
   D. wanted to show Ms. Kline that
      she could do the job.

10. How did Luz feel about the Dream
    Garden at the end of the first day?
    F. not willing to give up on it
    G. relieved that it was almost done
    H. ready to give up
    J. happy to have so much help

11. What happened at the lot just before
    Ms. Kline came back to check Luz's
    progress?
    A. Luz saw Rosie walk by.
    B. Someone planted a tulip.
    C. The neighbors had a party.
    D. Someone dumped garbage.

12. Which sentence shows how the
    neighbors felt about Luz when she
    gave Ms. Kline a dollar?
    F. "I figure lots of people will
       stop by and help."
    G. "Everybody crowds around,
       shaking my hands and clapping
       me on the back."
    H. "Mrs. Kline sounds like she can
       hardly believe it."
    J. "Everybody laughs, and the
       man looks a little confused."

13. The hardest part about getting the
    garden started was—
    A. cleaning up the trash.
    B. ordering from the catalog.
    C. planting seeds and trees.
    D. finding water.

14. When did most people in this story
    become truly interested in helping
    with the garden?
    F. on the first Saturday that Luz
       got started
    G. when Ms. Kline warned Luz to
       find more help
    H. when someone dropped
       garbage in the cleaned lot
    J. after the truck delivered the
       plants and supplies

15. Which is the best reason to think
    that the garden will be a success?
    A. Officers Ramirez and Carter
       will go to the celebration.
    B. Ali will let the group use his
       water.
    C. Rosie didn't join the group.
    D. The people in the neighborhood
       believe in it.

STOP

Compare and Contrast

Directions: Read the story. Then read each question about the story. Choose the best answer to each question. Mark the letter for the answer you have chosen.

Flowers and Vegetables

A famous poet once said, "My love is like a red, red rose."

I enjoy that poem because I also think red roses are beautiful. That's why I grow them in my garden.

My brother, Jesse, doesn't like flowers. He grows vegetables in *his* garden—peas, carrots, lettuce, and string beans. Jesse says that vegetables growing in a garden are the most beautiful sight on Earth.

Both Jesse and I enjoy working in our gardens. Our favorite time is early in the morning, when the weather is cool and dew covers every leaf.

This summer, I will enter my roses in the flower show. Maybe I'll win first place! Jesse doesn't like to enter contests, but he's just as proud of his peas and carrots as I am of my roses.

1. In the line, "My love is like a red, red rose," the poet compares—
   A. love to a flower.
   B. love to a garden.
   C. a rose to a garden.
   D. flowers to vegetables.

2. Both the narrator and the poet quoted—
   F. like roses.
   G. don't like roses.
   H. grow vegetable gardens.
   J. write poems.

3. One thing the narrator and Jesse have in common is that they both—
   A. like vegetables.
   B. like flowers.
   C. grow gardens.
   D. enter contests.

4. The clue word in the fourth paragraph that shows a comparison is—
   F. favorite.
   G. both.
   H. early.
   J. gardens.

5. One word that describes both Jesse and the narrator is—
   A. hard-working.
   B. lazy.
   C. foolish.
   D. cruel.

Notes for Home: Your child compared and contrasted elements in a short story. *Home Activity:* Think of two favorite activities that your child enjoys doing. Ask him or her to tell you some ways they are alike and ways that they are different.

Phonics: Consonant Sounds for *c* and *g*

Directions: Read the words in each box. Follow the instructions below.

1. Write the two words with the **hard-c** sound like **cat.**

   _____, _____

2. Write the two words with the **soft-c** sound like **cell.**

   _____, _____

> celebrate
> community
> nice
> panic

3. Write the part of each word that has the **hard-c sound.**

   _____, _____

4. Write the part of each word that has the **soft-c sound.**

   _____, _____

> practice
> convince

5. Write the two words with the **hard-g** sound like **get.**

   _____, _____

6. Write the two words with the **soft-g** sound like **gym.**

   _____, _____

> giant
> garden
> vegetable
> big

7. Write the part of each word that has the **hard-g** sound.

   _____, _____

8. Write the part of each word that has the **soft-g** sound.

   _____, _____

> garage
> garbage

9. Write the part of each word that has a hard consonant sound.

   _____, _____

> grocery
> courage

10. Write the part of each word that has a soft consonant sound.

    _____, _____

Notes for Home: Your child practiced distinguishing between hard and soft sounds for the letters *c* and *g*. **Home Activity:** Play a game of "I Spy." For example, say, "I spy something that begins with a hard *c*, as in *cat.*" Have your child find the object and say the name.

Technology: Locate/Collect Information/Telephone Directory

A **telephone directory** lists phone numbers and addresses for individual people and businesses. The **white pages** list entries for individuals and businesses in alphabetical order. The **yellow pages** list entries for businesses and advertisements by category or type of business.

You can also find phone numbers and addresses in "yellow pages" on the Internet. You can search for businesses on the Internet by category, such as garden supplies.

Directions: Write the category you would use to search the Internet for each store.

_____ **1.** a store that sells games and jump ropes

_____ **2.** a store that sells food

_____ **3.** a store that sells windows, doors, and lumber

_____ **4.** a store that sells baseball bats, basketballs, and sneakers

5. Look at the following categories. Write an **X** next to the category you would search to find a store that sells seeds, potting soil, and a spray to control weeds.

_____ Lawn Mowing Equipment

_____ Lawn and Garden Decorations

_____ Lawn and Garden Supplies

Name_____

When you choose a category on the Internet Yellow Pages, a listing is displayed. For gardening supplies, it might look like this:

Directions: Use the listings above to answer these questions.

6. You want to find out if a store sells what you are looking for without going there. What information could you use?

_____

_____

7. Which store is in Roxbury? _____

8. Which store is on Silver Rd.? _____

9. On the Internet, you can click on underlined words to get more information. What do you think you will get when you click on "map"?

_____

_____

10. How is searching the Internet Yellow Pages similar to searching the yellow pages in a phone book?

_____

_____

Notes for Home: Your child learned how to find a business on a yellow pages Web site. *Home Activity:* Ask your child to find a specific local store on a yellow pages Web site or in the yellow pages of a phone book.

Text Structure

- **Text structure** is the way a piece of writing is organized. The two main kinds of writing are fiction and nonfiction.
- **Fiction** tells stories of imaginary people and events. Events are often told in the order in which things happen.
- **Nonfiction** tells of real people and events or tells information about the real world. One way to organize nonfiction is to have a main idea followed by supporting details. Other ways to organize nonfiction are cause and effect, problem and solution, and comparison and contrast.

Directions: Reread "Your Best Friend." Then complete the table. Tell what kind of writing it is, list details from the piece, and determine how the piece is organized.

Title	"Your Best Friend"
Fiction or Nonfiction?	1.
1st Heading	2.
Detail	3.
Detail	4.
2nd Heading	5.
Detail	6.
Detail	7.
3rd Heading	8.
Detail	9.
Method of Organization	10.

Notes for Home: Your child read an article and identified text structure. *Home Activity:* Ask your child about some favorite books. Encourage him or her to identify text structure by telling you whether the material is fiction or nonfiction and by saying how it is organized.

Vocabulary

Directions: Choose the word from the box that best completes each sentence. Write the word on the matching numbered line below.

There are many different **1.** _____ of pigs. Many people are **2.** _____ of the small ones because they make good pets. Unlike guinea pigs, real pigs aren't seen **3.** _____ on everything in sight. A mother pig is called a **4.** _____, and father pigs are called **5.** _____ .

<table>
<tr><td colspan="3">**Check the Words You Know**</td></tr>
<tr><td>__ boars</td></tr>
<tr><td>__ fond</td></tr>
<tr><td>__ gnawing</td></tr>
<tr><td>__ sow</td></tr>
<tr><td>__ varieties</td></tr>
</table>

1. _____   4. _____

2. _____   5. _____

3. _____

Directions: Choose the word from the box that best matches each clue. Write the word in the puzzle.

Down

6. kinds

7. female pig

9. liking

Across

8. male pigs

10. biting away

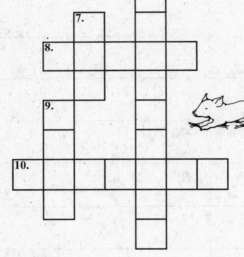

Write an Animal Care List

Imagine you are the proud owner of a guinea pig. On a separate sheet of paper, make a list of things you need to know to take care of your guinea pig. Use as many of the vocabulary words as you can.

Notes for Home: Your child has learned new vocabulary words from *I Love Guinea Pigs*. *Home Activity:* Talk with your child about the fun and responsibilities of having a pet. Encourage him or her to use the vocabulary words.

Text Structure

- **Text structure** is the way a piece of writing is organized.
- Fiction tells stories of imaginary people and events. They are usually told in the order in which things happen. Nonfiction tells of real people and events or tells information about the real world. Some ways to organize nonfiction are cause and effect, problem and solution, or comparison and contrast.

Directions: Reread the part of *I Love Guinea Pigs* where the author explains why guinea pigs are "sensible animals." Then answer the questions below.

They don't like the cold, of course, or the damp, any more than you would, and they're not happy living in a poky little place, any more than you would be. But as long as they have a comfortable, warm, dry place to live, guinea pigs are as happy as can be.

They're hardy animals and don't often get sick. Properly cared for, they can live a long time.

I once had a crested sow named Zen. She lived two years with me and then eight more with one of my daughters. People's hair grows whiter as they age, but Zen's grew darker.

Guinea pigs need plenty of food. They love eating, just like you do. . . .

From I LOVE GUINEA PIGS. Text Copyright © 1994 by Dick King-Smith. Illustrations Copyright © 1994 by Anita Jeram. Published by Candlewick Press, Cambridge, MA. Reproduced by permission of Walker Books Limited, London.

1. Is this text fiction or nonfiction? Tell why you think so.

_____

2. Name three ways that guinea pigs are compared to humans.

_____

_____

3. Name one way that guinea pigs are contrasted to humans.

_____

4. Tell two things that make guinea pigs happy.

_____

5. On a separate sheet of paper, tell how the author organized the text. Give another example from the story of how he used this text structure.

Notes for Home: Your child looked at how an excerpt of a larger text was organized. *Home Activity:* Find two or three of your child's favorite books and ask your child to tell you whether they are fiction or nonfiction. Discuss how each book is organized.

1.	Ⓐ	Ⓑ	Ⓒ	Ⓓ
2.	Ⓕ	Ⓖ	Ⓗ	Ⓙ
3.	Ⓐ	Ⓑ	Ⓒ	Ⓓ
4.	Ⓕ	Ⓖ	Ⓗ	Ⓙ
5.	Ⓐ	Ⓑ	Ⓒ	Ⓓ
6.	Ⓕ	Ⓖ	Ⓗ	Ⓙ
7.	Ⓐ	Ⓑ	Ⓒ	Ⓓ
8.	Ⓕ	Ⓖ	Ⓗ	Ⓙ
9.	Ⓐ	Ⓑ	Ⓒ	Ⓓ
10.	Ⓕ	Ⓖ	Ⓗ	Ⓙ
11.	Ⓐ	Ⓑ	Ⓒ	Ⓓ
12.	Ⓕ	Ⓖ	Ⓗ	Ⓙ
13.	Ⓐ	Ⓑ	Ⓒ	Ⓓ
14.	Ⓕ	Ⓖ	Ⓗ	Ⓙ
15.	Ⓐ	Ⓑ	Ⓒ	Ⓓ

Selection Test

Directions: Choose the best answer to each item. Mark the letter for the answer you have chosen.

Part 1: Vocabulary

Find the answer choice that means about the same as the underlined word in each sentence.

1. There are many <u>varieties</u> of cats.
   A. problems or fears
   B. habits or ways
   C. favorite foods or treats
   D. kinds or sorts

2. Henry counted seven <u>boars</u>.
   F. nests made by animals
   G. male pigs or hogs
   H. sounds made by pigs
   J. pens for small pets

3. The dog was <u>gnawing</u> on a box.
   A. biting and wearing away
   B. burrowing into
   C. batting or hitting lightly
   D. sniffing at

4. Liam decided to take the <u>sow</u>.
   F. smallest piglet in a litter
   G. piglet born in the winter
   H. fully grown female pig
   J. pig with several colors

5. The pet is <u>fond</u> of its owner.
   A. free or without need
   B. having a liking for
   C. growing tired or bored
   D. seeming afraid

Part 2: Comprehension

Use what you know about the selection to answer each item.

6. Guinea pigs belong to the same family as—
   F. horses.
   G. humans.
   H. pigs.
   J. mice.

7. The first guinea pigs came from—
   A. Australia.
   B. South America.
   C. Africa.
   D. Asia.

8. The author thinks that guinea pigs are—
   F. loud and active.
   G. shy and nervous.
   H. chubby and cuddly.
   J. fussy and messy.

9. How does the author know so much about guinea pigs?
   A. He had them as pets for much of his life.
   B. He studied them in pet shops.
   C. He read many books about guinea pigs.
   D. He is an animal doctor.

GO ON

10. Which sentence tells how this selection is written?
- F. It explains how someone solved a problem.
- G. It gives facts and opinions.
- H. It lists many events in the order they happened.
- J. It describes imaginary people and animals.

11. A guinea pig will become friendly and tame if its owner—
- A. holds and pets it often.
- B. keeps it in a cool, dry place.
- C. lets it go outdoors often.
- D. feeds it many different foods.

12. How were the guinea pigs named Beach Boy and King Arthur alike?
- F. They were both a bright golden color.
- G. They both lived to an old age.
- H. They were both buried in the yard.
- J. They both loved dandelions and clover.

13. Most of the details given in this selection are used to—
- A. compare baby and adult guinea pigs.
- B. describe the author's favorite guinea pig.
- C. explain how to feed a guinea pig that won't eat.
- D. tell what it is like having guinea pigs for pets.

14. Which detail is an opinion?
- F. A guinea pig sow carries her litter for about seventy days.
- G. The guinea pigs are born with their eyes open.
- H. Their mouths are already filled with teeth.
- J. Newborn guinea pigs are a funny sight.

15. What does the author want you to remember most about guinea pigs?
- A. how long they have been kept as pets
- B. how much pleasure they can give
- C. how much they are like other rodents
- D. how hard they are to care for

STOP

© Scott Foresman 4

Fact and Opinion

Directions: Read the passage. Then read each question about the passage. Choose the best answer to each question. Mark the letter for the answer you have chosen.

Down with Cats!

Cats make terrible pets!

First of all, as everyone knows, cats are hunters. They are related to lions and tigers. Today's house cats hunt mice, birds, and lizards just the way big cats hunt bigger animals.

Some people think this is a good quality. But I definitely do not. I feel sorry for the mice that my brother's cat tries to catch. Of course, my brother's cat has never yet caught a single mouse. But someday I believe he might!

Finally, dogs are much nicer than cats. That is not just my opinion. It's a fact!

1. In the first sentence, the writer gives—
   A. an order.
   B. a question.
   C. a statement of fact.
   D. a statement of opinion.

2. Which clue word in this sentence signals that it is an opinion? "Some people think this is a good quality."
   F. think   H. some
   G. good   J. is

3. A statement from the story that cannot be proved true or false is—
   A. cats are hunters.
   B. they are related to lions and tigers.
   C. dogs are much nicer than cats.
   D. house cats hunt mice, birds, and lizards.

4. The third paragraph includes—
   F. only statements of fact.
   G. statements of both fact and opinion.
   H. only statements of opinion.
   J. statements of fact that cannot be proved.

5. Which is **not** a good way to prove that one of the facts is true or false?
   A. Check an encyclopedia.
   B. Check a book about animals.
   C. Ask a friend.
   D. Ask an animal expert.

Notes for Home: Your child identified statements of opinions and facts in a passage. *Home Activity:* Ask your child to explain the difference between opinion and fact. Then take turns making statements about a subject, such as the weather, and identifying it as opinion or fact.

Word Study: Compound Words

Directions: Compound words are words made by joining two words, such as **sun + shine = sunshine.** Some compound words have a hyphen. Read this paragraph. Circle each compound word. Then write the word on the line.

Throughout history, people have had dogs as pets. Some dogs have long fur. They are called long-coated. Others have short fur. They are called smooth-coated. Newborn puppies have very little fur, so it is hard to tell how long their fur will be when they are grown-up dogs.

1. _____

2. _____

3. _____

4. _____

5. _____

Directions: Match each word in the first column with a word in the second column to make a compound word that makes sense. Write the word on the line.

6. snow   –legged   _____

7. four   storm   _____

8. any   times   _____

9. what   born   _____

10. new   out   _____

11. some   –haired   _____

12. through   ever   _____

13. long   way   _____

Directions: Choose two of the compound words you made. Write a sentence using each of your words.

14. _____

15. _____

Notes for Home: Your child wrote compound words. *Home Activity:* Look for compound words on directions that come with toys or games. Write each part of the word on separate slips of paper, then have your child put the words together.

Chart/Table

A **chart** organizes information in a way that is easy to follow. A **table** is a kind of chart that presents information in rows and columns.

Directions: Use the table to answer the questions that follow.

GUIDE TO GUINEA PIG CARE

Topics	What You Need to Know
Food and Water	Guinea pigs should eat a diet of hay, pellets, fresh fruit, and vegetables such as broccoli, cauliflower, carrots, and peas. Guinea pigs need lots of fresh water daily.
Bedding	Put some shredded newspaper at the bottom of the cage. Replace with fresh newspapers daily. You can also use towels and blankets but these have to be washed every day.
Vet Visits	Guinea pigs should have a physical exam twice a year. They should also see a vet if they have a loss of appetite, bleeding, diarrhea, hair loss, or show strange behavior.
Safety	Don't put plastic toys in a guinea pig's cage. It will chew them and could choke on the pieces.

1. Which row would you look at to find out what a guinea pig needs for sleeping?

_____

2. How can you use the table to find out if plastic toys are safe for guinea pigs?

_____

3. What four vegetables are good for a guinea pig's diet? _____

_____

4. What information can you learn by reading the section on Vet Visits?

_____

5. Suppose you were going to add another row to the table on what a guinea pig's sounds mean. What words would you use to label this topic?

_____

Directions: Study the table below. Use the table to answer the questions that follow.

"WHAT IS MY GUINEA PIG TRYING TO SAY TO ME?"

Guinea Pig Sounds	What It Probably Means
gurgles, grunts	comfort, happiness
squeaks, squeals	fear, in pain, hungry
cooing	calm, relaxed
hisses, teeth clacking	fighting, warning

6. If your guinea pig was grunting and cooing, what "Sounds" would you look under to learn more?

_____

7. If you saw a guinea pig clacking its teeth, how could you use this table to figure out what this means?

_____

_____

8. What sound could you expect from a guinea pig that does not want to be disturbed?

_____

9. Suppose you are adding a third column to this chart. It will tell how to respond to a guinea pig's sounds. What heading could you give this column?

_____

10. Why are headings in a table useful? _____

_____

_____

Notes for Home: Your child used tables to answer questions about pet care. **Home Activity:** Create a table with your child to keep track of weekly activities. For example, on Monday, your child might play soccer; on Tuesday, your child may watch a specific TV program, and so on.

Theme

• **Theme** is the underlying meaning of a story—a "big idea" that stands on its own outside the story.

1. Reread "The Swimming Hole." Write its theme on the line below.

_____

Directions: Read the story. Then answer the questions below.

> Ever since Malcolm could remember, Uncle Dave had kept his promises. One day, Uncle Dave broke a promise. He said he would come visit on Malcolm's birthday, and he didn't. Malcolm felt terrible. "I can never trust him again," he thought. The next time Uncle Dave visited, he said he was sorry. He had written down the wrong date on his calendar.
>
> Malcolm thought he could never trust Uncle Dave again. But his mother said, "Sometimes people do mean things, but sometimes they just make mistakes."
>
> "I guess he just made a mistake," said Malcolm. "So I guess I will try trusting him again."

2. Why did Malcolm always trust Uncle Dave?

_____

3. What does Uncle Dave do to make Malcolm stop trusting him?

_____

4. What does Uncle Dave do to show that Malcolm can trust him again?

_____

5. Use what you know about the events and characters of the story above to write about its theme. Below the theme, list all the details in the story that support this big idea. Use a separate sheet of paper.

Notes for Home: Your child has read a story and identified its theme, or big idea, as well as some details that support that theme. *Home Activity:* Talk together about a favorite book, movie, or television show. Invite your child to explain its theme, or "big idea."

Name_____

1.	Ⓐ	Ⓑ	Ⓒ	Ⓓ
2.	Ⓕ	Ⓖ	Ⓗ	Ⓙ
3.	Ⓐ	Ⓑ	Ⓒ	Ⓓ
4.	Ⓕ	Ⓖ	Ⓗ	Ⓙ
5.	Ⓐ	Ⓑ	Ⓒ	Ⓓ
6.	Ⓕ	Ⓖ	Ⓗ	Ⓙ
7.	Ⓐ	Ⓑ	Ⓒ	Ⓓ
8.	Ⓕ	Ⓖ	Ⓗ	Ⓙ
9.	Ⓐ	Ⓑ	Ⓒ	Ⓓ
10.	Ⓕ	Ⓖ	Ⓗ	Ⓙ
11.	Ⓐ	Ⓑ	Ⓒ	Ⓓ
12.	Ⓕ	Ⓖ	Ⓗ	Ⓙ
13.	Ⓐ	Ⓑ	Ⓒ	Ⓓ
14.	Ⓕ	Ⓖ	Ⓗ	Ⓙ
15.	Ⓐ	Ⓑ	Ⓒ	Ⓓ

Context Clues

> • When you are reading and you see an unfamiliar word, use **context clues,** or words around the unfamiliar word, to figure out its meaning.
> • The context may give a definition or an explanation. Often the definition or explanation comes just before or just after the word. Sometimes a synonym, a word with nearly the same meaning as another word, is used as a context clue.

Directions: Reread "Crocodilians." Then complete the table. Use the context clues in the article to figure out the meaning of each word in the table.

Word	Meaning
osteoderms	1.
hides	2.
amphibious	3.
ripple	4.
ectothermic	5.

Notes for Home: Your child used context clues to figure out the meanings of five words. *Home Activity:* Encourage your child to use context clues to figure out the meanings of unfamiliar words as you read together.

Vocabulary

Directions: Cross out the word that does not belong in each group.

1. roam   wander   dash   travel

2. armor   shell   scales   elbow

3. reptile   snakes   chickens   alligators

Directions: Choose the word from the box that best completes each sentence. Write the word on the matching numbered line to the right.

Check the Words You Know
__ armor
__ fierce
__ harshest
__ lizards
__ prey
__ reptiles
__ roam

My friend Carrie told me a story about some
4. _____ and scary dragons. She said that the climate where they live is one of the 5. _____ in the world. The dragons have hard scales, like 6. _____, to protect them. They 7. _____ the land in search of animals to eat. The dragons are strong and swift, so they almost always catch their 8. _____.

"I bet they are not even dragons. I bet they are only 9. _____," I said.

"Well, maybe not," said Carrie. "But some 10. _____ are lizards that are so large that they look like dragons."

4. _____

5. _____

6. _____

7. _____

8. _____

9. _____

10. _____

Write a Science Log

Imagine you are a scientist who studies reptiles. Write an entry in your log describing one of the reptiles you are studying. What does it look like? How does it act? What foods does it eat? Use as many vocabulary words as you can in your logs.

Notes for Home: Your child identified and used new words from *Komodo Dragons*. **Home Activity:** Talk with your child about different types of reptiles, such as snakes, lizards, turtles, or alligators. Create a picture encyclopedia. Write captions for each picture.

© Scott Foresman 4

Context Clues

- When you are reading and see an unfamiliar word, use **context clues,** or words around the unfamiliar word, to figure out its meaning.
- **Context clues** include definitions, explanations, and synonyms (words that have the same or nearly the same meaning as other words).

Directions: Reread the part of *Komodo Dragons* that talks about where Komodo dragons live. Then answer the questions below. Look for context clues as you read.

Komodo dragons are a type of lizard called a *monitor.* They come from the Komodo Island area of Indonesia, near the northwest shore of Australia. It is one of the harshest and hottest places in the world. Often, the temperature is over 100° F. Sometimes it even gets as hot as 110° F.

On the hottest days, dragons escape the heat by getting out of the sun. They rest in underground burrows. But in the morning, when they first wake up, they lie in the sun to warm up. They do that on cooler days, too. That is because, like all lizards, they are **reptiles.** Reptiles are **cold-blooded** animals. They need outside heat (like sunlight) to warm them up.

From KOMODO DRAGONS by Thane Maynard. Copyright © 1997 by The Child's World, Inc. Reprinted by permission. All rights reserved.

1. What is a *monitor?* _____

2. What sentence in the passage contains a clue to the meaning of *monitor?*

_____

3. What does *cold-blooded* mean?

_____

4. What sentence in the passage contains a clue to the meaning of *cold-blooded?*

_____

_____

5. Read the section called "What Do Komodo Dragons Eat?" Find an unfamiliar word in that section and define it on a separate sheet of paper. Tell what context clue helped you figure out the word's meaning.

Notes for Home: Your child practiced using context clues in a story. *Home Activity:* Think of a difficult word, and tell your child a sentence that makes its meaning clear ("Today I saw a bird called a *flamingo.*"). Ask your child to tell you what the word means.

1.	(A)	(B)	(C)	(D)
2.	(F)	(G)	(H)	(J)
3.	(A)	(B)	(C)	(D)
4.	(F)	(G)	(H)	(J)
5.	(A)	(B)	(C)	(D)
6.	(F)	(G)	(H)	(J)
7.	(A)	(B)	(C)	(D)
8.	(F)	(G)	(H)	(J)
9.	(A)	(B)	(C)	(D)
10.	(F)	(G)	(H)	(J)
11.	(A)	(B)	(C)	(D)
12.	(F)	(G)	(H)	(J)
13.	(A)	(B)	(C)	(D)
14.	(F)	(G)	(H)	(J)
15.	(A)	(B)	(C)	(D)

Selection Test

Directions: Choose the best answer to each item. Mark the letter for the answer you have chosen.

Part 1: Vocabulary

Find the answer choice that means about the same as the underlined word in each sentence.

1. Scott wrote a report on reptiles.
   A. plants found in the desert
   B. mammals of South America
   C. types of building materials
   D. cold-blooded animals

2. The lion followed its prey.
   F. an animal hunted for food
   G. an animal's parents
   H. the way an animal behaves
   J. a smell left behind by an animal

3. Jamal caught two lizards.
   A. common illnesses
   B. hard balls used in a game
   C. kinds of reptiles with four legs
   D. insects with wings

4. Talia's cat likes to roam.
   F. wander
   G. hunt
   H. sleep
   J. hide

5. Tigers are fierce hunters.
   A. patient
   B. savage; wild
   C. restless
   D. skillful; clever

6. This has been the harshest winter ever.
   F. warmest
   G. mildest; most pleasant
   H. longest
   J. roughest; most difficult

7. That animal's skin is like armor.
   A. a thick hairy coat
   B. a band worn around the waist
   C. a covering worn to protect the body
   D. a kind of saddle

Part 2: Comprehension

Use what you know about the selection to answer each item.

8. Komodo dragons are—
   F. make-believe animals.
   G. alligators.
   H. birds.
   J. lizards.

9. Where do Komodo dragons live?
   A. Australia
   B. India
   C. Indonesia
   D. Africa

GO ON

10. Komodo dragons swish their tails back and forth to—

   F.   show they like something.

   G. smell the air around them.

   H. hold on to their prey.

   J.   help them balance.

11. How is the female Komodo dragon different from the male?

   A. She is usually smaller.

   B. She is not as strong.

   C. She digs burrows.

   D. She is active during the day.

12. What word is being defined in this sentence? "That's why the tongue is forked, or shaped like a Y."

   F.   shaped

   G. forked

   H. tongue

   J.   why

13. Because Komodo dragons are cold-blooded, they—

   A. prefer to eat warm food.

   B. must escape the heat by getting out of the sun.

   C. need outside heat to warm them up.

   D. can easily live in very cold places.

14. You can tell that Komodo dragons are—

   F.   well suited to their surroundings.

   G. very particular about what they eat.

   H. not very intelligent animals.

   J.   lazy because they sleep all day.

15. Which sentence states an opinion?

   A. Dragon eggs have a soft, smooth shell.

   B. Hatching takes about eight months.

   C. Komodo dragons live on only a few islands.

   D. Komodo dragons are very interesting creatures.

STOP

© Scott Foresman 4

Main Idea and Supporting Details

REVIEW

Directions: Read the passage. Then read each question about the passage. Choose the best answer to each question. Mark the letter for that answer.

Animals of the Arctic

Animals that live in the Arctic have found many ways to cope with the cold.

Polar bears have two main guards against the cold: extra fur and a layer of fat. These things help keep bears warm in below-freezing temperatures.

Some animals have other ways of handling the cold. Hares and reindeer can run quickly across the snow. That's because their wide "snowshoe" feet don't break through the snow's crust.

Hares in the Arctic also have very small ears. That's because body heat escapes through the ears, cooling the body down. Smaller ears allow less heat to escape.

Some animals, such as whales, birds, and caribou, handle the cold by heading south. They live in the Arctic in the summer, when temperatures are higher.

1. A key word to the main idea in the second paragraph is—
   A. fat.
   B. fur.
   C. guards.
   D. layer.

2. A detail in the third paragraph is—
   F. whales head south.
   G. snowshoe feet don't break through the crust.
   H. hares and reindeer.
   J. hares have small ears.

3. A key word to the main idea of the third paragraph is—
   A. hares.
   B. reindeer.
   C. run.
   D. break.

4. A key word to the main idea in the last paragraph is—
   F. south.
   G. whales.
   H. birds.
   J. caribou.

5. The main idea of the whole passage is that Arctic animals—
   A. get cold.
   B. leave during the winter.
   C. have small ears.
   D. find ways to cope with cold.

Notes for Home: Your child practiced identifying the main idea and its supporting details in a story. *Home Activity:* Ask your child to name an important family rule (main idea), such as washing hands before dinner. Have him or her give examples of why the rule is important.

© Scott Foresman 4

Phonics: *r*-Controlled Vowels

Directions: Many vowels have a different sound when they are followed by the letter **r.** Listen to the difference in **cat** and **cart.** Read each sentence below. Each sentence has a word with a vowel followed by the letter **r.** Write the word on the line. Underline the **r-controlled vowel** you hear and see in the word.

_____ **1.** Many animals in the wild have sharp claws.

_____ **2.** An animal's fur protects it from the cold.

_____ **3.** Many wild animals today have to fight against human progress to survive.

_____ **4.** It is sometimes not wise to live too near wild animals.

_____ **5.** The birth of a wild animal in captivity is often a great accomplishment.

_____ **6.** One should be cautious around wild animals who seem curious about people.

_____ **7.** Some animals come out at night, protected by the dark.

_____ **8.** The deer come out at night to eat the leaves off low-hanging trees.

_____ **9.** I could sit and watch these animals for hours.

Directions: Read the words in the box. Some words have the same vowel sound as **for.** Other words have the same vowel sound as **word.** Write each word in the correct column.

for	**word**	north
10. _____	13. _____	armor
11. _____	14. _____	shore
12. _____	15. _____	born
		predator
		monitor

Notes for Home: Your child listened for words where the letter *r* changes the sound of the vowel that precedes it, such as *start, morning, shirt,* and *curious.* **Home Activity:** Read a book about animals with your child. Have your child look for words with these sounds.

Encyclopedia

An **encyclopedia** gives general information about many different subjects. Encyclopedias are organized in a set of **volumes,** or books, usually in alphabetical order. An **entry** is an encyclopedia article. Entries are listed in alphabetical order. An **entry word** is the word or phrase that begins each entry and tells its subject. To find information in an encyclopedia, use a **key word** that identifies the information you are trying to find.

Directions: Use this encyclopedia entry about Komodo Island to answer the questions that follow.

KOMODO ISLAND has only one village and fewer than 500 people. The Komodo Island National Park takes up most of the space on Komodo Island.

Many of the mountains on the island were formed by volcanoes. These volcanic mountains are usually brown and lifeless. Every year, however, during monsoon season, these mountains appear green. This color comes from small tropical plants that grow on the hill slopes.

Komodo Island is one of the few places left on Earth where the Komodo dragon can be found. About 1,000 Komodo dragons live there. Komodo dragons are giant monitor lizards that run wild on the island. They can grow to up to 10 feet long, weigh up to 300 pounds, and live for 100 years.

---

1. What key word would someone have looked up to find this article?

_____

2. Would the entry above appear before or after an entry on Koala bears? Explain.

_____

_____

_____

3. What key word would you use to find more information about monsoons?

_____

4. What key word would you use to find information about volcanoes?

_____

5. Suppose you have a volume of an encyclopedia marked "M." Name two entry words you might find in this volume.

_____

Name _____

Directions: Read the encyclopedia entry about reptiles. Use the entry to answer the questions that follow.

REPTILES are a group of animals that include snakes, lizards, turtles, crocodiles, the tuatara, and many extinct creatures. The bodies of many snakes are covered with scales. Reptiles can be found in temperate and tropical climates around the world. They are cold-blooded animals, so most of them cannot live in polar regions.

Reptile behavior. Most reptiles lay eggs, but many lizards and snakes give birth to live offspring. When the winter is cold, some reptiles *estivate*—this means they become inactive. Most reptiles rely on the sun's heat to stay warm.

---

6. Would you expect to find an article about tigers before or after the reptiles entry in the encyclopedia? Explain.

_____

_____

7. What key word would you use to find out more about snakes?

_____

8. What section of the entry contains information about how reptiles act?

_____

9. What letter would likely be on the volume of the encyclopedia that contains this entry on reptiles?

_____

10. If you wanted to get information about the reptile exhibit at your local zoo, would an encyclopedia be a good reference source? Explain.

_____

_____

Notes for Home: Your child read encyclopedia entries and answered questions about them. *Home Activity:* Brainstorm questions about related topics. Ask your child to tell the key words he or she would use to look up more information in an encyclopedia.

Making Judgments

- **Making judgments** means thinking about and deciding how to react to people, situations, and ideas in a story.

Directions: Reread this description of John Henry smashing the boulder. Then answer the questions below. Support each answer with story details.

"Don't see how you can do what dynamite couldn't," said the boss of the crew.

John Henry chuckled. "Just watch me." He swung one of his hammers round and round his head. It made such a wind that leaves blew off the trees and birds fell out of the sky.

RINGGGGGG!

The hammer hit the boulder. That boulder shivered like you do on a cold winter morning when it looks like the school bus is never going to come.

RINGGGGGG!

The boulder shivered like the morning when freedom came to the slaves.

From JOHN HENRY by Julius Lester. Copyright © 1994 by Julius Lester. Used by permission of Dial Books for Young Readers, a division of Penguin Putnam Inc.

1. What do you think the crew boss thinks of John Henry?

_____

_____

2. How do you think John Henry feels about his own abilities?

_____

3. What is one way you can tell that *John Henry* is a legend?

_____

_____

4. Do you think the comparison, "That boulder shivered like you do on a cold winter morning when it looks like the school bus is never going to come" is a good one?

_____

_____

5. On a separate sheet of paper, write a description of the kind of person you think John Henry is. Include details from the story.

 Notes for Home: Your child used story details to make judgments about a story and its characters. **Home Activity:** Have your child choose a character from a book or a TV show and make judgments about the character's behavior, using details from the work.

1.	Ⓐ	Ⓑ	Ⓒ	Ⓓ
2.	Ⓕ	Ⓖ	Ⓗ	Ⓙ
3.	Ⓐ	Ⓑ	Ⓒ	Ⓓ
4.	Ⓕ	Ⓖ	Ⓗ	Ⓙ
5.	Ⓐ	Ⓑ	Ⓒ	Ⓓ
6.	Ⓕ	Ⓖ	Ⓗ	Ⓙ
7.	Ⓐ	Ⓑ	Ⓒ	Ⓓ
8.	Ⓕ	Ⓖ	Ⓗ	Ⓙ
9.	Ⓐ	Ⓑ	Ⓒ	Ⓓ
10.	Ⓕ	Ⓖ	Ⓗ	Ⓙ
11.	Ⓐ	Ⓑ	Ⓒ	Ⓓ
12.	Ⓕ	Ⓖ	Ⓗ	Ⓙ
13.	Ⓐ	Ⓑ	Ⓒ	Ⓓ
14.	Ⓕ	Ⓖ	Ⓗ	Ⓙ
15.	Ⓐ	Ⓑ	Ⓒ	Ⓓ

Technology: Card Catalog/Library Database

To find books in the library, you can use the **card catalog** or **library database.** You can search for a book by author, title, or subject. When searching by author, always use the last name first.

Directions: The computer screen shows how to search a library database. Tell how you would search to find each of the following books. Write **A** for author, **T** for title, or **S** for subject.

_____ **1.** a book by Kathryn Lasky

_____ **2.** a book about tall tales

_____ **3.** a book titled *Me and My Hero*

_____ **4.** a book about steam drills

_____ **5.** a book by Julius Lester

Library books are sorted by call numbers, usually based on the Dewey Decimal System. Books of fiction have call numbers that use letters from the last names of the authors. They are sorted alphabetically. Books that are nonfiction are sorted by numbers and appear in a different section from fiction books.

Directions: The computer screen shows the results of a subject search on *tall tales*. Use the results to answer the questions that follow.

Subject/Titles	Call Number
Tall Tales—Fiction	
1) Paul and Babe	EAT
2) The Great North Wind	THR
Tall Tales—Characters	
3) Paul Bunyan and Other Tall Tale Heroes	839.1
Tall Tales—Authors	
4) Julius Lester: A Master Storyteller	860.8

Type a number to find out more about each title. ☐

Type **A, T,** or **S** to begin a new search. ☐

6. Which books listed are books of fiction? _____

_____

7. What does the call number THR represent? _____

_____

8. Will *Paul and Babe* be on the shelf before or after *The Great North Wind?* Explain.

_____

9. Which of the two nonfiction books listed would be first on a shelf? Explain.

_____

_____

10. Which book will be about someone who writes and tells tall tales?

_____

Notes for Home: Your child answered questions about a card catalog/library database. **Home Activity:** Take your child to the library. Have your child show how to use the card catalog or library database to find a book he or she might like to read.

Drawing Conclusions

- Authors don't always tell you everything. Instead, they may give you a few details about what happens or about characters.
- You can use the details and what you know to **draw conclusions,** or figure out things about people or animals and what they do.

Directions: Reread "Winter of the Snowshoe Hare." Then complete the table. Write a conclusion for each piece of evidence given. Write evidence that supports each conclusion drawn.

Evidence (Story Details and What I Know)	Conclusions
The sounds of paws and breathing are louder.	1.
The master blew the whistle.	2.
The dog turned and trotted back to the master.	3.
4.	The hare didn't know the dog had turned back.
5.	The hare was safe.

Notes for Home: Your child read a story and used story details and life experience to draw conclusions. ***Home Activity:*** Watch a television show or a movie with your child. Discuss what conclusions you can draw about how the characters feel or why they behave as they do.

Vocabulary

Directions: Choose the word from the box that best matches
each definition. Write the word on the line.

_____ 1. large, fierce, North American bear

_____ 2. pancakes

_____ 3. a measure of wood

_____ 4. railroad or bus station

_____ 5. wooden-framed shoes

Directions: Read the letter. Choose the word from the box that best
completes each sentence. Write the word on the matching numbered
line to the right.

Dear Charlie,

   We have just arrived at the train **6.** _____
in the mountains. The snow is so deep we
might need **7.** _____ to get around! Grandma
says we get to stack a whole **8.** _____ of
wood. Then we'll be hungry for her great
9. _____ ! I hope we get to see a **10.** _____
bear on this trip. That would be amazing!

                    Love,
                    Beth

6. _____

7. _____

8. _____

9. _____

10. _____

Write a Letter

On a separate sheet of paper, write a
letter to a friend—real or imaginary—who lives in the Great North Woods. Show
your excitement about going to visit your friend. Use as many vocabulary words as
you can.

Notes for Home: Your child identified and used vocabulary words from *Marven of the Great
North Woods.* **Home Activity:** With your child, use the vocabulary words to make up an
adventure story about camping in the woods.

Name _____

Drawing Conclusions

- As you read, use story details and what you know to **draw conclusions,** or make a sensible decision, about the characters and what they do.

Directions: Reread this passage from *Marven of the Great North Woods* in which Marven is becoming used to the logging camp. Then answer the questions below.

> Every day Marven worked until midday, when he went into the cookhouse and ate baked beans and two kinds of pie with Mr. Murray and the cook. After lunch he returned to his office and worked until the jacks returned from the forest for supper.
>
> By Friday of the second week, Marven had learned his job so well that he finished early.
>
> He had not been on his skis since he had arrived at camp. Every day the routine was simply meals and work, and Marven kept to his office and away from the lumberjacks as much as he could. But today he wanted to explore, so he put on his skis and followed the sled paths into the woods.

Excerpt from MARVEN OF THE GREAT NORTH WOODS, copyright © 1997 by Kathryn Lasky Knight, reprinted by permission of Harcourt Brace & Company.

1. Why don't Marven and Mr. Murray eat with the lumberjacks?

_____

2. Why do you think Marven could learn his job so well in so little time?

_____

3. Why do you think Marven kept away from the lumberjacks?

_____

4. How does Marven feel about his daily routine? How do you know?

_____

_____

5. How do you think Marven feels about the lumberjacks by the end of the story? On a separate sheet of paper, explain your answer.

Notes for Home: Your child drew conclusions about characters and their actions. *Home Activity:* Have your child draw conclusions by playing a game of "If". For example: *If your dog whines by the front door, what do you think it wants? (to go outside)*

1.	Ⓐ	Ⓑ	Ⓒ	Ⓓ
2.	Ⓕ	Ⓖ	Ⓗ	Ⓙ
3.	Ⓐ	Ⓑ	Ⓒ	Ⓓ
4.	Ⓕ	Ⓖ	Ⓗ	Ⓙ
5.	Ⓐ	Ⓑ	Ⓒ	Ⓓ
6.	Ⓕ	Ⓖ	Ⓗ	Ⓙ
7.	Ⓐ	Ⓑ	Ⓒ	Ⓓ
8.	Ⓕ	Ⓖ	Ⓗ	Ⓙ
9.	Ⓐ	Ⓑ	Ⓒ	Ⓓ
10.	Ⓕ	Ⓖ	Ⓗ	Ⓙ
11.	Ⓐ	Ⓑ	Ⓒ	Ⓓ
12.	Ⓕ	Ⓖ	Ⓗ	Ⓙ
13.	Ⓐ	Ⓑ	Ⓒ	Ⓓ
14.	Ⓕ	Ⓖ	Ⓗ	Ⓙ
15.	Ⓐ	Ⓑ	Ⓒ	Ⓓ

Selection Test

Directions: Choose the best answer to each item. Mark the letter for the answer you have chosen.

Part 1: Vocabulary

Find the answer choice that means about the same as the underlined word in each sentence.

1. The hunters saw a <u>grizzly</u>.
   - A. kind of tree
   - B. large, fish-eating bird
   - C. kind of wild cat
   - D. large, fierce kind of bear

2. Do you like <u>flapjacks</u>?
   - F. pancakes
   - G. a game played with cards
   - H. tools for lifting
   - J. rabbits

3. Grant bought a <u>cord</u> of logs.
   - A. a long flat-bottomed sled
   - B. a certain amount of cut wood
   - C. a thin, strong rope
   - D. a box used to store things

4. The hikers wore <u>snowshoes</u>.
   - F. heavy boots lined with fur
   - G. long, narrow runners for gliding on snow
   - H. skates with metal blades
   - J. light frames worn on the feet for walking in deep snow

5. Tom met us at the <u>depot</u>.
   - A. small restaurant
   - B. camp
   - C. train station
   - D. hotel

Part 2: Comprehension

Use what you know about the selection to answer each item.

6. Marven spent four months at a—
   - F. music camp.
   - G. sports camp.
   - H. logging camp.
   - J. hunting camp.

7. Marven's job was to—
   - A. keep the payroll.
   - B. stack wood in the office.
   - C. ring the morning bell.
   - D. make breakfast.

8. On the first morning, Marven ran to the bunkhouse to—
   - F. find an overcoat to wear.
   - G. talk with Jean Louis.
   - H. light the lamps.
   - J. make sure the men were up.

GO ON

9. In this selection, you can tell that
   "*Lève-toi!*" means—
   A. Get up!
   B. You're lazy!
   C. It's time for breakfast!
   D. Good morning!

10. You can tell that Marven was—
    F. glad to be away from his family.
    G. stronger than Jean Louis.
    H. good with numbers.
    J. afraid of snow.

11. Which word best describes Marven
    in his job?
    A. bored
    B. organized
    C. lazy
    D. patient

12. When he skied across the lake,
    Marven began to cry because—
    F. the rest of his family had died.
    G. Jean Louis was laughing at
       him.
    H. his hands and feet were frozen.
    J. he felt alone and afraid.

13. How did Jean Louis feel about
    Marven?
    A. He thought Marven was a pest.
    B. He did not like taking care of
       him.
    C. He came to love him almost as
       a son.
    D. He thought Marven acted like a
       baby.

14. When Marven didn't see his family
    at the train station, he probably
    thought that—
    F. he was at the wrong stop.
    G. they had forgotten him.
    H. he should go back to the woods.
    J. everyone had died from the flu.

15. How did Marven's experience away
    from home change him?
    A. He was forced to grow up faster
       than most children his age.
    B. He began to depend on others
       to take care of him.
    C. He became afraid to get close
       to others because they would
       die.
    D. He realized he didn't really
       need his family.

STOP

Context Clues

Directions: Read the story. Then read each question about the story. Choose the best answer to each question. Mark the letter for the answer you have chosen.

A Friend to Many

Frank Benson wanted to improve life for everyone in Hillsdale. His many projects helped countless people he never even met. Because Frank felt that everyone should be literate, he started a program to teach people who couldn't read. He also founded a Library on Wheels program that brought books to people living out in the country. It was the first program of its kind in the state.

When Frank passed away at the age of 92, a memorial service was held at the town's main library. Many family members and friends told stories about all the good things Frank had done in his life. Later, the town voted to rename the library after Frank. The brass plaque on the front door reads, "Frank Benson: A Friend to Many."

1. The word <u>countless</u> in this passage means—
   A. many.
   B. few.
   C. poor.
   D. mean.

2. The word <u>literate</u> in this passage means able to—
   F. make money.
   G. read.
   H. litter.
   J. teach.

3. The word <u>founded</u> in this passage means—
   A. find.
   B. purchased.
   C. started.
   D. approved.

4. The word <u>memorial</u> in this passage means something done to—
   F. get a person elected to office.
   G. raise funds for a good cause.
   H. make people happy.
   J. remember a person who has died.

5. The word <u>plaque</u> in this passage means—
   A. a door.
   B. a sign.
   C. a wooden board.
   D. a book.

Notes for Home: Your child defined words in a story using context clues. **_Home Activity:_** Give your child a list of unfamiliar words. Use each word in a sentence and challenge your child to use context clues to figure out the meaning of each unfamiliar word.

Word Study: Regular Plurals

Directions: To make most nouns plural, add the letter **-s.** For nouns that end in **x, s, ss, ch,** or **sh,** add **-es.** For nouns that end in **consonant** and **y,** add **-es.** Read the paragraph below. Make each word in ( ) plural. Write the plural word on the line.

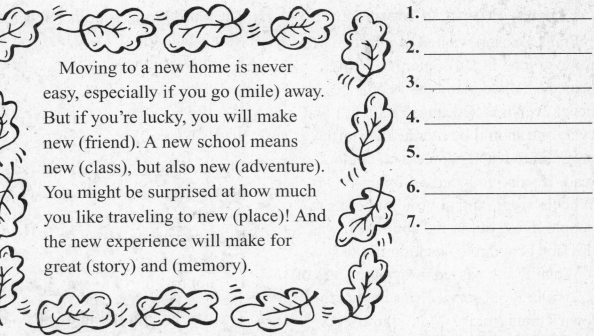

Moving to a new home is never easy, especially if you go (mile) away. But if you're lucky, you will make new (friend). A new school means new (class), but also new (adventure). You might be surprised at how much you like traveling to new (place)! And the new experience will make for great (story) and (memory).

1. _____
2. _____
3. _____
4. _____
5. _____
6. _____
7. _____

Directions: Write the plural form for each word. For some words, you will add **-s.** For some you will add **-es.** You may need to change some letters before adding **-es.**

8. pencil _____
9. candy _____
10. ax _____
11. city _____
12. monkey _____
13. lunch _____
14. paper _____
15. tower _____
16. glass _____

17. bush _____
18. tree _____
19. star _____
20. fox _____
21. horse _____
22. flapjack _____
23. beard _____
24. shadow _____
25. pony _____

Notes for Home: Your child changed singular nouns into plurals by adding *-s* or *-es* to create words such as *tigers, babies,* and *boxes.* **Home Activity:** Read some coupons with your child. Look for plural words. Talk about how the singular noun changed to become a plural noun.

Locate/Collect Information

To find out information about a subject, you can use resources such as books, magazines, newspapers, dictionaries, encyclopedias, videotapes, audiotapes, CD-ROMs, Internet Web sites, photographs, drawings, and diagrams. You can also talk to a reference librarian or an expert in the field.

Directions: Review these resources for information on lumberjacking. Use the resources to answer the questions that follow.

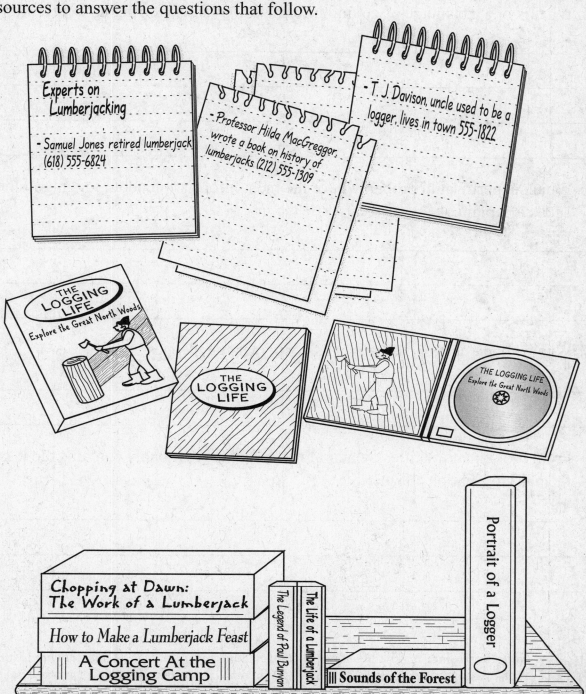

Name _____

1. If you wanted to find out what the lumberjacks ate for dinner, which resources do you think would be most helpful?

_____

_____

_____

2. What is one advantage of getting information by interviewing an expert?

_____

_____

_____

3. Which expert would probably have the most information about logging in the 1800s? Explain.

_____

_____

_____

4. What is one question you might ask expert Samuel Jones?

_____

_____

5. From looking at the titles, which of the audiotapes probably contains the least factual information? Explain.

_____

_____

_____

 Notes for Home: Your child learned about using different resources. ***Home Activity:*** List five adults your child knows. Ask your child to tell you on what subject each person could be interviewed as an expert, such as Louisa—flowers, Chico—biology.

Generalizing

- A **generalization** is a broad statement or rule that applies to many examples.
- Often clue words like *all, most, many, some, sometimes, usually, seldom, few,* or *generally* signal generalizations. A **valid generalization** is supported by facts and your own knowledge. A **faulty generalization** is not.

Directions: Reread "Salmon for All." Write **V** if the generalization is valid. Write **F** if it is faulty. Give evidence from the text to support your choices.

Generalization	V or F	Evidence
Many animals eat salmon.	V	Bears, foxes, birds, and people all eat salmon.
Foxes sometimes feed their pups salmon.	1.	2.
Bears never eat salmon.	3.	4.
Bears always hide their tracks.	5.	6.
There is seldom enough salmon for everyone.	7.	8.
Not everyone can catch salmon.	9.	10.

Notes for Home: Your child identified valid and faulty generalizations. ***Home Activity:*** Take turns using the clue words listed above to make generalizations. (*I* <u>seldom</u> *am wrong.*) Determine whether each generalization is valid (accurate) or faulty (not accurate).

Vocabulary

Directions: Choose the word from the box that best completes each sentence. Write the word on the line to the left.

_____ **1.** Did you know that a ranch is often known by a set of _____, or letters?

_____ **2.** Every steer in the ranch's whole _____ is marked with these letters.

_____ **3.** The young _____ are separated from the mother cows to be marked.

_____ **4.** Even the horses standing in the _____ have been marked.

_____ **5.** Cowboys groom their horses by brushing their _____.

Directions: Choose the word from the box that best matches each clue. Write the word in the puzzle.

Down

6. to mark with a hot iron

7. straps held by a horse's rider

8. pen where horses or cattle are kept

Across

9. large number of one kind of animal

10. straps that fit on horses' heads

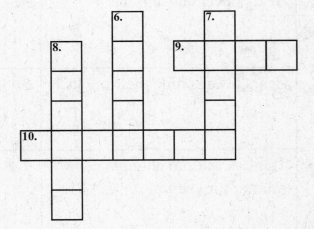

Write a Postcard

On a separate sheet of paper, write a short postcard to a friend telling about a visit to a ranch. Use as many of the vocabulary words as you can.

Notes for Home: Your child identified and used vocabulary words from *On the Pampas*.
Home Activity: With your child, find out more about life on a modern ranch. Use as many of the vocabulary words as possible as you and your child discuss what you have learned.

Generalizing

- Sometimes when you read, you are given ideas about several things or people. When you make a statement about all of them together, you are making a **generalization.**
- A **valid generalization** is accurate. A **faulty generalization** is not accurate.

Directions: Reread this passage from *On the Pampas*. Then make generalizations based on what you read.

> At noon, everybody would sit down around one big table and eat together. I was always hungry. Grandma, Susanita's mother, and María the cook had been working hard all morning too. They would make soup, salad, and lamb stew or pot roast, or my favorite, *carbonada,* a thick stew made of corn and peaches.
>
> After lunch the grown-ups took a *siesta,* but not us. We liked to stay outdoors. Some afternoons, when it was too hot to do anything else, we rode out to a eucalyptus grove that was nice and cool, and stayed there until it got dark, reading comic books or cowboy stories.
>
> From ON THE PAMPAS by María Cristina Brusca, © 1991 by María Cristina Brusca. Reprinted by permission of Henry Holt and Company, LLC.

1. What was true of mornings on the ranch?

_____

2. What usually happened at noon?

_____

3. What did all the grown-ups do after lunch?

_____

4. What did the children do after lunch?

_____

5. On a separate sheet of paper, write a valid generalization about life on the *pampas.*

Notes for Home: Your child used details to make generalizations about a story. *Home Activity:* Read a story or newspaper article with your child. Together, make generalizations— statements about several things or people in the story.

Name_____

1.	Ⓐ	Ⓑ	Ⓒ	Ⓓ
2.	Ⓕ	Ⓖ	Ⓗ	Ⓙ
3.	Ⓐ	Ⓑ	Ⓒ	Ⓓ
4.	Ⓕ	Ⓖ	Ⓗ	Ⓙ
5.	Ⓐ	Ⓑ	Ⓒ	Ⓓ
6.	Ⓕ	Ⓖ	Ⓗ	Ⓙ
7.	Ⓐ	Ⓑ	Ⓒ	Ⓓ
8.	Ⓕ	Ⓖ	Ⓗ	Ⓙ
9.	Ⓐ	Ⓑ	Ⓒ	Ⓓ
10.	Ⓕ	Ⓖ	Ⓗ	Ⓙ
11.	Ⓐ	Ⓑ	Ⓒ	Ⓓ
12.	Ⓕ	Ⓖ	Ⓗ	Ⓙ
13.	Ⓐ	Ⓑ	Ⓒ	Ⓓ
14.	Ⓕ	Ⓖ	Ⓗ	Ⓙ
15.	Ⓐ	Ⓑ	Ⓒ	Ⓓ

Selection Test

Directions: Choose the best answer to each item. Mark the letter for the answer you have chosen.

Part 1: Vocabulary

Find the answer choice that means about the same as the underlined word in each sentence.

1. Helen walked to the <u>corral</u>.
   - A. building for storing hay
   - B. piece of land planted with crops
   - C. small country store
   - D. pen where animals are kept

2. Marco grabbed the <u>reins</u>.
   - F. seat for a rider
   - G. straps used to guide a horse
   - H. loops for a rider's foot
   - J. long rope with a loop on the end

3. The <u>herd</u> headed west.
   - A. group of animals of one kind
   - B. great mass of clouds
   - C. group of sailing ships
   - D. line of covered wagons

4. Where are the <u>bridles</u> stored?
   - F. hats with wide brims
   - G. strong leather pants
   - H. part of a harness for a horse
   - J. metal shoes for horses

5. She brushed the horses' <u>manes</u>.
   - A. back part of a horse's body
   - B. parts of the mouth
   - C. long heavy hair on a horse's neck
   - D. place for an animal in a barn

6. Maria helped <u>brand</u> the cattle.
   - F. mark by burning with a hot iron
   - G. move to another location
   - H. gather into a group
   - J. give food and water to

7. The boys saw some <u>calves</u>.
   - A. plants with no leaves
   - B. large, flat rocks
   - C. dark storm clouds
   - D. young cows or bulls

8. Whose <u>initials</u> are these?
   - F. first letters of a person's names
   - G. coverings for the hands
   - H. marks made by the tip of a finger
   - J. sets of funny drawings

GO ON

Part 2: Comprehension

Use what you know about the selection to answer each item.

9. The ranch where the author spent the summer was called—
   A. San Enrique.
   B. La Carlota.
   C. Buenos Aires.
   D. La Gauchita.

10. Susanita is the author's—
    F. cousin.
    G. grandmother.
    H. horse.
    J. friend.

11. What is a *ñandú?*
    A. a horse
    B. a herd of cattle
    C. a kind of bird
    D. a fancy belt

12. Based on this selection, which generalization is most likely true?
    F. All horses are friendly.
    G. Few cattle live on the pampas.
    H. Girls always learn faster than boys.
    J. Most gauchos work very hard.

13. What can you tell about the author of this story?
    A. She is willing to try new things.
    B. She doesn't really have what it takes to be a gaucho.
    C. She is secretly jealous of Susanita.
    D. She likes to call attention to herself.

14. The author's grandmother expects her to—
    F. write to her during the winter.
    G. take her horse home with her.
    H. come back the next summer.
    J. share her horse with Susanita.

15. The author probably feels proudest that she—
    A. stole a bird's egg.
    B. had become a gaucho.
    C. baked a birthday cake for Grandma.
    D. escaped from the ñandú.

STOP

Context Clues

Directions: Read the story. Then read each question about the story. Choose the best answer to each question. Mark the letter for the answer you have chosen.

Life on a TV Ranch

I've never set foot on an actual ranch, but I've traveled to many in my mind. That's because TV shows made life on a ranch so enticing. It looks like so much fun.

One thing confused me about cowboy shows. I wasn't sure of the era when they were taking place.

They all showed herds of cattle and corrals. But in one they got water from a well and cooked on a wood-burning stove. In another there was a modern kitchen. In one there were cars. In another, there were only horses.

It took me a while to realize the obvious truth: Some cowboy shows took place in the Old West. Some took place in the present.

1. The word <u>actual</u> in the story means—
   A. working.
   B. nasty.
   C. make-believe.
   D. real.

2. The word <u>enticing</u> in the story means—
   F. dangerous.
   G. appealing.
   H. uninviting.
   J. boring.

3. The word <u>confused</u> in the story means—
   A. puzzled.
   B. dazzled.
   C. angered.
   D. entertained.

4. Which phrase gives a clue to the meaning of <u>era</u>?
   F. wasn't sure
   G. when they were taking place
   H. one thing confused me
   J. they all showed

5. An <u>obvious</u> truth is—
   A. sad.
   B. unclear.
   C. clear.
   D. whole.

Notes for Home: Your child defined words using context clues. **_Home Activity:_** Read a magazine or newspaper article with your child. Discuss which words are unfamiliar and what context clues can be used to figure out their meanings.

Word Study: Inflected Forms with
-ed, -ing, -es

Directions: You can change a verb by adding endings, such as **-ed, -ing,** or **-es.** For some verbs, you don't need to change the base word when you add these endings. For other verbs, you might need to drop the final **e,** change a **y** to **i,** or double the final consonant. Add **-ed** and **-ing** to each base word. Write the new words on the lines.

**Verbs That
Don't Change**   **-ed**   **-ing**

stay   1. _____   2. _____

turn   3. _____   4. _____

**Verbs That Drop
the Final e**   **-ed**   **-ing**

chase   5. _____   6. _____

graze   7. _____   8. _____

**Verbs That Double
the Final Consonant**   **-ed**   **-ing**

stop   9. _____   10. _____

drag   11. _____   12. _____

Directions: If the verb ends in **consonant** and **y,** change the **y** to **i** before adding **-ed** or **-es.** Keep the **y** before adding **-ing.** Add **-ed, -ing,** and **-es** to the word **try.**

13. try + -ed = _____

14. try + -ing = _____

15. try + -es = _____

Notes for Home: Your child added *-ed, -ing,* and *-es* to verbs. *Home Activity:* Read a story with your child. Help your child find verbs with these endings.

Name _____

Evaluate Information/Draw Conclusions

When you research information, you need to **evaluate** it to see if the information is accurate and up-to-date. You also need to make sure it meets the needs of your project. For example, a newspaper article might be up-to-date, but it may not have the information you need. When you find information you can use, you need to **draw conclusions** about it by deciding for yourself what the information means.

Directions: Read this encyclopedia entry about cattle. Use the information to answer the questions that follow.

Cattle: The Global Picture

In 1995, there were about $1\frac{1}{4}$ billion beef and dairy cattle in the world. More than one third of the cattle are raised in Asia. Many millions more are raised in South America. India has more cattle than any other country in the world, but the demand for meat in India is low because many people there believe that the cow is a sacred animal.

A century ago, there were 60 million cattle in the United States. In the early 1990s, the U.S. Department of Agriculture estimated that this number had grown to close to 100 million. During this same time period, each American ate about 67 pounds of beef a year and drank about 100 quarts of milk.

© Scott Foresman 4

1. If you wanted to find information about the topic "Life on the Range," would this encyclopedia article be useful? Explain.

_____

_____

2. Would this encyclopedia article be considered "up-to-date" if you were trying to find out about the number of cattle in the world currently? Explain.

_____

_____

_____

3. About how many pounds of beef does an American eat each year? About how much milk does an American drink each year? Why do you think data about milk consumption was given?

_____

_____

_____

4. According to the entry, in which country are cows treated as sacred animals? Where did you find this information?

_____

5. Would you say that the information presented would help you prepare a report on fast food in America? Why?

_____

_____

_____

Notes for Home: Your child read an encyclopedia entry to gather information and draw conclusions about it. *Home Activity:* Discuss with your child ways to find out more information about a particular topic. Talk about what resources would have useful content.

Predicting

- To **predict** means to tell what you think might happen next in a story or article based on what has already happened. Your prediction is what you say will happen next.
- Predicting is a process of checking and changing your predictions as you read, based on new information.

Directions: Reread "Summer Surfers." Fill in the prediction table. For each story event, tell what logical predictions can be made based on what you have read up to that point in the story. One prediction has been done for you.

What Happened	What Might Happen
Ben and the seal surfed side by side.	Ben and the seal will become friends.
Ben couldn't take his eyes off the seal.	1.
Ben fell off his board and struck a rock.	2.
Ben was forced upward and saw sunlight again.	3.
The seal flipped Ben onto his board.	4.
Once he caught his breath, Ben felt fine.	5.

Notes for Home: Your child read a story and used story details and life experience to make predictions about what will happen next in a story. *Home Activity:* Watch a favorite TV show with your child. During the commercial breaks, predict what will happen next.

Vocabulary

Directions: Choose the word from the box that best completes each sentence.
Write the word on the matching numbered line to the right.

One of the worst kinds of storms is a
1. _____. When a bad storm is coming,
the long, loud **2.** _____ of an alarm
sounds a warning. During the last
storm, we hid in the cellar. My dog
Floppy pressed close and **3.** _____ me
the whole time. He was scared too!
Having him near me was **4.** _____ and
comforting. After the storm passed, I
5. _____ him to come out of the cellar
by offering him a biscuit.

1. _____

2. _____

3. _____

4. _____

5. _____

Check the Words You Know
__ accident
__ coaxed
__ nuzzled
__ soothing
__ tornado
__ wail

Directions: Cross out the word that does not belong
in each group.

6. accident	disaster	plan	crash
7. wail	shout	scream	whisper
8. tornado	hurricane	breeze	storm
9. soothing	calming	quieting	annoying
10. coaxed	demanded	begged	asked

Write a TV Weather Report

On a separate sheet of paper, write a TV weather report telling
listeners that a big storm is coming their way. Tell people what they
should do to stay safe. Use as many of the vocabulary words as
you can.

Notes for Home: Your child identified and used vocabulary words from *The Storm*. **Home Activity:** Talk with your child about bad storms and what to do in order to stay safe during one. Use as many vocabulary words as possible.

Predicting

- **Predicting** means telling what you think might happen next in a story or article, based on what has already happened.
- Your prediction can change as you read, based on new information.

Directions: Reread the passage from *The Storm*. Think about the predictions you made while reading. Answer the questions below based on reading this passage.

It was so incredible that for a moment he simply stared. From the rise of the farmyard he watched the snakelike funnel slowly twist across the distant fields and broaden into a larger blackness. Before his eyes it became a black wall headed straight for the farm. Fear replaced amazement. He hurried back across the lot. The wind was shrieking now. But before he could get to the house, he heard horses.

Looking back, there were Buster and Henry tearing madly around the inner lot. How could they have gotten out? He didn't know. And not just Buster, but Henry, pride and joy of his father. Jonathan couldn't think if he had time or not, if it was safe or not.

From THE STORM by Marc Harshman. Copyright © 1995 by Marc Harshman. Used by permission of Cobblehill Books, a division of Penguin Inc.

1. Does it seem likely that the tornado will strike the farm?

_____

2. Do you think Buster and Henry will go back into the barn by themselves?

_____

3. What might Jonathan do to help save Buster and Henry?

_____

4. What do you think might happen if Jonathan gets Buster and Henry back into the barn?

_____

5. As you read *The Storm,* what predictions did you make? Did any of your predictions change as you continued reading? Explain.

Notes for Home: Your child used story details to predict what will happen next. ***Home Activity:*** Name a situation (such as forgetting to turn off the bath water). Ask your child to predict what might happen next.

Name_____

1.	Ⓐ	Ⓑ	Ⓒ	Ⓓ
2.	Ⓕ	Ⓖ	Ⓗ	Ⓙ
3.	Ⓐ	Ⓑ	Ⓒ	Ⓓ
4.	Ⓕ	Ⓖ	Ⓗ	Ⓙ
5.	Ⓐ	Ⓑ	Ⓒ	Ⓓ
6.	Ⓕ	Ⓖ	Ⓗ	Ⓙ
7.	Ⓐ	Ⓑ	Ⓒ	Ⓓ
8.	Ⓕ	Ⓖ	Ⓗ	Ⓙ
9.	Ⓐ	Ⓑ	Ⓒ	Ⓓ
10.	Ⓕ	Ⓖ	Ⓗ	Ⓙ
11.	Ⓐ	Ⓑ	Ⓒ	Ⓓ
12.	Ⓕ	Ⓖ	Ⓗ	Ⓙ
13.	Ⓐ	Ⓑ	Ⓒ	Ⓓ
14.	Ⓕ	Ⓖ	Ⓗ	Ⓙ
15.	Ⓐ	Ⓑ	Ⓒ	Ⓓ

Name _____

Selection Test

Directions: Choose the best answer to each item. Mark the letter for the answer you have chosen.

Part 1: Vocabulary

Find the answer choice that means about the same as the underlined word in each sentence.

1. That was a coyote's <u>wail</u>.
   A. baby animal
   B. long, sad call
   C. wild animal's home
   D. mark made by a foot or paw

2. I <u>coaxed</u> the horse into the barn.
   F. trapped
   G. pushed from behind
   H. tied with a rope
   J. persuaded gently

3. We were caught in a <u>tornado</u>.
   A. fast-moving water
   B. trap for catching animals
   C. destructive, whirling wind
   D. sudden attack

4. Gus was in a bicycle <u>accident</u>.
   F. something harmful that happens unexpectedly
   G. important race
   H. parade
   J. repair shop

5. Alan was <u>soothing</u> the animals.
   A. exciting
   B. calming
   C. feeding
   D. gathering

6. The dog <u>nuzzled</u> Laura's hand.
   F. rubbed with the nose
   G. pushed away roughly
   H. took quick small bites
   J. looked at in a fearful way

Part 2: Comprehension

Use what you know about the story to answer each item.

7. What did Jonathan love?
   A. street noise
   B. trucks
   C. hot weather
   D. watching thunderstorms

8. How did Jonathan lose the use of his legs?
   F. He was hit by a truck.
   G. He was born that way.
   H. A tree fell on his legs.
   J. He fell off his bicycle.

GO ON

9. Jonathan's mom left the house to—
   A. buy a new car.
   B. have her car fixed.
   C. pick up Jonathan's dad.
   D. go food shopping.

10. When the wind rose and the sky turned a green-yellow color, you could predict that—
    F. the house would be ruined.
    G. there would be no storm.
    H. it would soon be night.
    J. a tornado was coming.

11. During the tornado, where was the safest place for Jonathan?
    A. in the root cellar
    B. inside the house
    C. outside in the yard
    D. under a tree

12. Jonathan probably cried when he found the rooster because he—
    F. had loved that bird.
    G. was worried about his parents.
    H. suddenly realized the same thing could have happened to him.
    J. knew his parents would be angry at him for leaving the animals.

13. You can tell from this story that tornadoes are—
    A. similar to snowstorms.
    B. very powerful and dangerous.
    C. impossible to escape from.
    D. nothing to be afraid of.

14. What bothered Jonathan most about being in a wheelchair?
    F. He could not play games.
    G. People saw his "condition" rather than the person he was.
    H. He could not feed the horses.
    J. He disliked having to ask other people for help.

15. As a result of his experience in the storm, Jonathan felt—
    A. guilty that he was not able to save the rooster.
    B. angry at his parents for leaving him alone during a storm.
    C. afraid that his parents would leave him alone again.
    D. better about himself and how others would see him.

STOP

Drawing Conclusions and Character

REVIEW

Directions: Read the story. Then read each question about the story. Choose the best answer to each question. Mark the letter for the answer you have chosen.

What You're Made Of

Jane's English cousins were visiting. When Jane said there was a tornado watch, Will asked if they'd watch it on TV.

"No, we have to watch *out* for one," Jane said gently.

"Should I stay by the window?" asked Violet.

"No," said Jane just as gently. But she frowned. "If it becomes a warning, then we have to go down to the shelter."

Two hours later, Jane led her cousins down to the shelter. "We'll wait out the storm here," she said. Will looked afraid. Jane put an arm around him.

"You'll be okay," she said in a soothing voice. "Show us what you're made of."

1. Will asked if he would watch the tornado on TV because—
   A. he was bored.
   B. he thought that's what Jane meant.
   C. nothing else was on.
   D. he was joking.

2. Why didn't Violet's idea make sense?
   F. It would be boring.
   G. Violet was too young to be the look-out.
   H. It would be dangerous.
   J. She wouldn't be able to see the tornado.

3. Why did Jane lead her cousins into the shelter?
   A. She was showing it off.
   B. The danger of the tornado had increased.
   C. The tornado hit the house.
   D. Everyone was bored.

4. When Jane answers gently, she shows she is—
   F. making fun of her cousins.
   G. insecure.
   H. afraid.
   J. kind.

5. Jane puts her arm around Will to try to—
   A. help him be less afraid.
   B. keep him from falling.
   C. make him go to the shelter.
   D. keep him from leaving.

Notes for Home: Your child drew conclusions about the characters in a story. *Home Activity:* Read or tell a story about someone who was brave. Ask your child to draw conclusions about the character and the character's actions.

Phonics: Consonant Sounds
/j/, /ks/, /kw/

Directions: The sound /j/ can be spelled **dge** or **ge** as in **ledge** or **change.** The sound /ks/ can be spelled **x** or **xc** as in **fox** or **except.** The sound /kw/ can be spelled **qu** as in **quick.** Read each word below. Sort each word by the sounds you hear. Write each word in the correct column.

| fidget | box | quiet | coaxed | huge |
| quite | sixty | ledge | explore | quilt |

/j/

1. _____

2. _____

3. _____

/ks/

4. _____

5. _____

6. _____

7. _____

/kw/

8. _____

9. _____

10. _____

Directions: Read each sentence. Listen for the word that has the consonant sounds /j/, /ks/, or /kw/. Write the word on the line. Circle the letters that represent that sound.

_____ **11.** The weather forecaster changed her report to include a tornado warning.

_____ **12.** The storm hit the edge of town.

_____ **13.** It was exciting to see the storm, but frightening too.

_____ **14.** Just as quickly as it had come up, the storm died out.

_____ **15.** People who saw the tornado tried to explain what it was like.

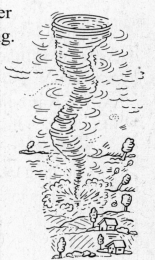

Notes for Home: Your child practiced identifying consonant sounds: **/j/** in *ledge* and *change,* **/ks/** in *fox* and *except,* and the **/kw/** in *quick.* **Home Activity:** Read a newspaper story with your child. Challenge your child to listen for words with these sounds and point them out.

Almanac

An **almanac** is a book that is published every year. It contains calendars, weather information, and dates of holidays. It also contains many charts and tables of current information about subjects such as city population and recent prize winners in science, literature, or sports.

Directions: Review this information from an almanac. Use the information to answer the questions that follow.

Tornado Facts

- The width of a tornado can vary from a few meters to a kilometer.
- Their "funnels" are made visible by dust that they suck up from the ground.
- Most tornadoes spin counterclockwise in the northern hemisphere and clockwise in the southern hemisphere.
- Tornado damage is caused by winds that often move at speeds of more than 300 miles per hour.

Notable U.S. Tornadoes Since 1980

Date	Location	Deaths
June 3, 1980	Grand Island, NE	4
March 2–4, 1982	South, Midwest	17
May 29, 1982	Southern IL	10
May 18–22, 1983	Texas	12
March 28, 1984	N. Carolina, S. Carolina	57
April 21–22, 1984	Mississippi	15

Measuring Tornadoes

Tornadoes are measured by the Fujita (or F) scale, created by T. Theodore Fujita. The F scale rates tornadoes on a scale of 0–5.

Rank	Wind Speed (mi/hr)	Damage	Strength
F-0	Up to 72 mi/hr	Light	Weak
F-1	73–112 mi/hr	Moderate	Weak
F-2	113–157 mi/hr	Considerable	Strong
F-3	158–206 mi/hr	Severe	Strong
F-4	207–260 mi/hr	Devastating	Violent
F-5	More than 261 mi/hr	Incredible	Violent

Name_____

1. If you wanted to know if a strong wind where you live was tornado strength, what section of the almanac page would you look at?

_____

2. Which notable tornado caused the greatest number of deaths? Give the date and location of this tornado. How is this information presented in the almanac?

_____

_____

_____

3. What information can you find about the size of tornadoes?

_____

_____

_____

4. If a tornado's wind speed is 200 mi/hr, what would the damage level be according to the Fujita scale?

_____

_____

_____

5. When might you want to use an almanac as a resource instead of an encyclopedia? Explain.

_____

_____

_____

_____

Notes for Home: Your child read and interpreted information about tornadoes found in an almanac. ***Home Activity:*** Look at an almanac together. Take turns sharing interesting and/or useful information you find.

Drawing Conclusions

- As you read, look at the details and make decisions about the characters and what happens in the story or article.
- When you make decisions about the characters or events, you are **drawing conclusions.**

Directions: Reread "Another Death on the Ranch." Then complete the table. Write a conclusion for each piece of evidence given. Write evidence that supports each conclusion drawn.

Evidence (Story Details and What I Know)	Conclusions
1.	Hank is proud of his job.
Hank doesn't consider the milk cow a suspect.	2.
3.	It will be difficult for Hank to solve the crime.
Hank goes to the chickenhouse and is deep in thought about the murder.	4.
5.	Hank feels unappreciated.

Notes for Home: Your child read a story and used story details and life experience to draw conclusions. ***Home Activity:*** Have your child observe a pet or a neighborhood animal and draw conclusions about the animal's behavior based on observation and experience.

Vocabulary

Directions: Cross out the word that does **not** belong in each group.

1. cobra	rattlesnake	alligator	garden snake
2. coiled	straight	curled	looped
3. lame	hurt	sure-footed	limping
4. plunged	dipped	dived	floated
5. triumph	success	victory	loss

Check the Words You Know

__ cobra
__ coiled
__ lame
__ plunged
__ triumph

Directions: Choose the word from the box that best matches each clue. Write the letters of the word on the blanks. The boxed letters spell something that is given as an award.

6. success

6. ___ ___ ___ ___ ☐ ___ ___

7. unable to walk properly

7. ___ ___ ___ ☐

8. wound around into a pile

8. ___ ___ ___ ___ ___ ☐

9. big, scary snake

9. ___ ___ ___ ☐ ___

10. threw with force

10. ___ ☐ ___ ___ ___ ___

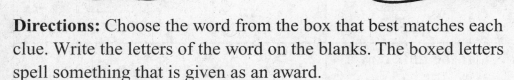

Something that is given as an award: ___ ___ ___ ___ ___

Write an Animal Story

On a separate sheet of paper, write a story in which the main character is an animal. Tell what problem your character faces and solves. Use as many vocabulary words as possible.

Notes for Home: Your child identified and used vocabulary words from *Rikki-tikki-tavi*. *Home Activity:* With your child, recall stories you have read or seen on TV about animals that have helped humans. Try to use vocabulary words as part of your discussion.

© Scott Foresman 4

Drawing Conclusions

- When you use details from the story and what you know to make decisions about the characters or events, you are **drawing conclusions.**

Directions: Reread this passage from *Rikki-tikki-tavi*. It takes place the morning after Rikki-tikki helped kill Nag. Then answer the questions below.

> When morning came, Rikki-tikki was very stiff but well pleased with himself. "Now I have Nagaina to deal with, and she will be worse than five Nags. And there's no knowing when the eggs will hatch. I must go see Darzee," he said.
>
> Without waiting for breakfast, Rikki-tikki ran to the thornbush where Darzee was singing a song of triumph at the top of his voice. The news of Nag's death was all over the garden, because his body had been put on the garbage heap.
>
> "Oh, you stupid tuft of feathers!" said Rikki-tikki. "Is this the time to sing?"
>
> From RIKKI TIKKI TAVI by Rudyard Kipling. Adapted and illustrated by Jerry Pinkney. Copyright © 1997 by Jerry Pinkney. By permission of Morrow Junior Books, a division of William Morrow & Company, Inc.

1. Why does Rikki-tikki expect Nagaina to "be worse than five Nags"?

_____

2. What eggs is Rikki-tikki talking about? What will happen when they hatch?

_____

3. Why does Rikki-tikki say, "I must go see Darzee"?

_____

4. Why doesn't Rikki-tikki think this is the time to sing?

_____

_____

5. On a separate sheet of paper, write a description of Rikki-tikki. Use details from the story to support your answer.

Notes for Home: Your child used story details to draw conclusions. ***Home Activity:*** Share events from work, a trip, and so on with your child. Provide details so your child can draw conclusions about why things happened or why somebody acted a certain way.

Name_____

1.	Ⓐ	Ⓑ	Ⓒ	Ⓓ
2.	Ⓕ	Ⓖ	Ⓗ	Ⓙ
3.	Ⓐ	Ⓑ	Ⓒ	Ⓓ
4.	Ⓕ	Ⓖ	Ⓗ	Ⓙ
5.	Ⓐ	Ⓑ	Ⓒ	Ⓓ
6.	Ⓕ	Ⓖ	Ⓗ	Ⓙ
7.	Ⓐ	Ⓑ	Ⓒ	Ⓓ
8.	Ⓕ	Ⓖ	Ⓗ	Ⓙ
9.	Ⓐ	Ⓑ	Ⓒ	Ⓓ
10.	Ⓕ	Ⓖ	Ⓗ	Ⓙ
11.	Ⓐ	Ⓑ	Ⓒ	Ⓓ
12.	Ⓕ	Ⓖ	Ⓗ	Ⓙ
13.	Ⓐ	Ⓑ	Ⓒ	Ⓓ
14.	Ⓕ	Ⓖ	Ⓗ	Ⓙ
15.	Ⓐ	Ⓑ	Ⓒ	Ⓓ

Selection Test

Directions: Choose the best answer to each item. Mark the letter for the answer you have chosen.

Part 1: Vocabulary

Find the answer choice that means about the same as the underlined word in each sentence.

1. The man caught a <u>cobra</u>.
   A. bad illness
   B. large cat with spots
   C. songbird
   D. poisonous snake

2. Art <u>plunged</u> into the lake.
   F. opened
   G. looked
   H. walked
   J. dived

3. Our game ended in <u>triumph</u>.
   A. victory or success
   B. loss or defeat
   C. a tie score
   D. sadness

4. The snake <u>coiled</u> itself.
   F. shed its skin
   G. wound around something
   H. unfolded
   J. slid away slowly

5. Terri's dog is <u>lame</u>.
   A. having fleas
   B. bad-tempered
   C. not able to walk right
   D. expecting puppies soon

Part 2: Comprehension

Use what you know about the story to answer each item.

6. What kind of animal is Chuchundra?
   F. a rat
   G. a muskrat
   H. a mongoose
   J. a snake

7. Nag believes that if he can rid the house of people, then—
   A. he and Nagaina can move in.
   B. Rikki-tikki will leave.
   C. a mongoose can live in the garden again.
   D. he can be crowned king.

8. Nag waits by the water jar to—
   F. take a drink.
   G. attack the man.
   H. catch Rikki-tikki.
   J. save the eggs.

GO ON

9. Darzee's wife pretends her wing is broken in order to—
   A. make Nagaina angry.
   B. lead the boy into a trap.
   C. save Rikki-tikki.
   D. trick Nagaina.

10. What can you tell about cobras from this story?
    F. Cobras are very dangerous.
    G. Most cobras can sing.
    H. Baby cobras like to eat melon.
    J. Adult cobras don't bite children.

11. How is Darzee's wife different from Darzee?
    A. She is a better singer.
    B. She has a broken wing.
    C. She is smarter.
    D. She is not as brave.

12. When Nagaina goes up on the porch, Rikki-tikki is—
    F. waiting by the bathroom drain.
    G. eating melons.
    H. destroying her eggs.
    J. looking for Nag.

13. Which word best describes Nagaina?
    A. hateful
    B. stupid
    C. careless
    D. shy

14. What was most important to Rikki-tikki?
    F. having a friend
    G. keeping Teddy safe
    H. sleeping in the house
    J. playing tricks on snakes

15. What part of this story could **not** really happen?
    A. A cobra lays her eggs in the garden.
    B. A bird sings loudly.
    C. A mongoose kills a snake.
    D. Animals talk to people.

STOP

Name _____

Making Judgments

REVIEW

Directions: Read the story. Then read each question about the story. Choose the best answer to each question. Mark the letter for the answer you have chosen.

Flo and Bob

"'Do this!' 'Don't do that!' That's all you say," cackled Flo the hen crossly to Bob the dog.

"Someday your life may depend on it," said Bob as he went to check on the ducks.

One day a fox appeared. Flo said, "Can I help you?"

"Just looking for now," answered the fox.

That night there was a loud squawking in the henhouse. Bob ran to see what was the matter. A fox!

"Help!" cried Flo. "What should we do?"

"Join wings so the fox can't grab any one of you," said Bob. "Leave him to me."

The hens did what Bob said. Bob chased the fox away. Flo never again complained about Bob's orders.

1. Bob is—
   A. mean.
   B. angry.
   C. careful.
   D. silly.

2. Flo is—
   F. helpful.
   G. annoyed.
   H. gentle.
   J. strong.

3. When the fox says "Just looking," he means that—
   A. he is not sure what he wants.
   B. he wants to find Bob.
   C. he is figuring a way into the henhouse.
   D. he wants to make friends with the hens.

4. In the story, Bob—
   F. is afraid.
   G. is mean.
   H. ignores the chickens.
   J. knows that there are dangers in the world.

5. By the end of the story, Flo has—
   A. decided to leave the henhouse.
   B. learned her lesson.
   C. lost a friend.
   D. complained to the fox.

Notes for Home: Your child made judgments about characters and events in a story. **Home Activity:** Watch a TV show with your child. Invite him or her to make judgments about events and characters. Prompt your child by asking, *Is that a nice way to act? Was that smart?*

Word Study: Base Words

Directions: Many words are made by adding letters to the beginning or end of a word. The word you start with is called the **base word.** Read each word below. Find the base word for each word. Write it on the line.

1. hidden _____

2. sensible _____

3. emptied _____

4. frightened _____

5. forgotten _____

6. mournful _____

7. tingled _____

8. gently _____

9. lowered _____

10. misspelled _____

11. beautifully _____

12. recalled _____

Directions: Base words can help you figure out the meaning of new words. Read each sentence. Think about the base word for the underlined word. Then read the two definitions in ( ). Circle the correct definition.

13. The small animals were frightened by the snake. (awakened/scared)
14. The sensible thing for a hunted animal to do is to stay with a group. (foolish/smart)
15. The bird searched for hidden dangers. (out of sight/out in the open)
16. But the animals had forgotten about the family in the house. (kept in mind/ not remembered)
17. They let out a mournful cry as they thought about the family's fate. (bright/sad)
18. The boy tingled with fear as he faced the snake. (a stinging feeling/a sleepy feeling)
19. The mongoose told the snake he had emptied the nest of all its eggs. (left nothing/filled up)

Directions: Write a sentence using the word **courageous.** If you're not sure what the word means, use the base word to help you.

20. _____

Notes for Home: Your child found base words in longer words, such as *care* in *carefully*. **Home Activity:** Read a magazine article with your child. As you spot longer words with base words, say, for example, "I spy the base word *near.*" Have your child find the longer word.

Schedule

A **schedule** is a special kind of chart that tells you when events take place. For example, arrival and departure times for buses and trains are often organized in schedules.

Directions: Read the schedule. Use it to answer the questions that follow.

The Sun Prairie News is proud to sponsor:
Animal Rescue Stories
Meet the animals who saved their owners' lives.
Hear the amazing tales by the animals' owners.

Schedule of Presentations
(Each presentation will last 45 minutes.)

Saturday, October 3	9:00 A.M.	Mark and his dog, Pudding
	11:00 A.M.	Tonya and her cat, Pink Paws
	3:00 P.M.	J.T. and his monkey, Tippy
Sunday, October 4	11:00 A.M.	Miguel and his ferret, Freddy
	2:00 P.M.	Mark and his dog, Pudding
	3:30 P.M.	Carla and her cat, Detour

Program held in the F.W. Richey Auditorium,
100 State St., Sun Prairie, WI (920) 555-2304

1. What are the names of the animals who are part of the first and last presentations of the weekend? List the times and dates when these two animals will appear.

_____

_____

_____

2. Which owner and animal will be presenting twice? What are your choices in dates and times to see them?

_____

_____

_____

3. What two owners will be presenting at 11:00 A.M. each day?

_____

_____

_____

4. If you arrived at the auditorium at 2:00 P.M. on Saturday, October 3, which presentations could you see that day? Explain.

_____

_____

_____

5. How long will Tonya and Pink Paws' presentation be? How do you know?

_____

_____

_____

Notes for Home: Your child used a schedule to find dates and times of special presentations. *Home Activity:* Find examples of schedules you and your child use often, such as TV listings or a bus schedule. Take turns asking each other questions about the schedule.

Paraphrasing

- **Paraphrasing** is explaining something in your own words. A paraphrase should keep the author's meaning.
- A paraphrase should include all of the author's ideas, but it should be easier to read than the original.

Directions: Reread "Blue Jay Takes the Heat." Then complete the table. Paraphrase the sentence or sentences from the story that are listed in the first column. Write your paraphrase of the text in the second column.

Author's Sentences	My Paraphrase
Paragraph 1, Sentence 2	1.
Paragraph 1, Last two sentences	2.
Paragraph 4, First sentence	3.
Paragraph 4, Sentences 2–5	4.
Last paragraph, Last sentence	5.

Notes for Home: Your child read a story and paraphrased parts of it in his or her own words. *Home Activity:* Give your child some directions, such as asking for a particular can from a cupboard. Ask your child to restate the directions simply, using his or her own words.

Vocabulary

Directions: Choose the word from the box that best matches each definition. Write the word on the line.

_____ 1. proposed

_____ 2. good-bys

_____ 3. too proud of one's own looks or abilities

_____ 4. threw with force; past tense of *fling*

_____ 5. worn by members of a group on duty

_____ 6. confused, twisted

Directions: Choose the word from the box that best completes each sentence. You will use some words more than once. Write the word on the line to the left.

_____ 7. Last night's wind had _____ leaves and branches all around the yard.

_____ 8. Lydia _____ that we check the weather report to see if it would rain today.

_____ 9. "This afternoon is our band concert, and our _____ might get wet," she said.

_____ 10. Just to be safe, Lydia grabbed her umbrella as she said her _____.

Write a Description

On a separate sheet of paper, write a description of a storm. Use as many vocabulary words as you can.

Notes for Home: Your child identified and used vocabulary words from *Half-Chicken*. **Home Activity:** Have your child give a synonym (a word with the same or nearly the same meaning as another word) for each vocabulary word (*good-bys, farewells*).

Paraphrasing

- **Paraphrasing** is explaining something in your own words. A paraphrase should include all of the author's ideas, but it should be easier to read than the original.

Directions: Reread what happens in *Half-Chicken* when the half-chicken hatches out of the egg. Then follow the instructions below.

Finally there was a tiny sound. The baby chick was pecking at its egg from the inside. The hen quickly helped it break open the shell, and at last the thirteenth chick came out into the world.

Yet this was no ordinary chick. He had only one wing, only one leg, only one eye, and only half as many feathers as the other chicks.

It was not long before everyone at the ranch knew that a very special chick had been born.

The ducks told the turkeys. The turkeys told the pigeons. The pigeons told the swallows. And the swallows flew over the fields, spreading the news to the cows. . . .

From MEDIOPOLLITO/HALF-CHICKEN by Alma Flor Ada. Copyright Text © 1995 by Alma Flor Ada. Illustrations 1995 by Kim Howard. Used by permission of Delacorte Press, a division of Random House, Inc.

1. Paraphrase the first paragraph.

_____

2. Paraphrase the second paragraph.

_____

3. Paraphrase the third paragraph.

_____

4. Paraphrase the fourth paragraph.

_____

5. Reread the passage. Then, on a separate sheet of paper, paraphrase the entire passage in your own words.

Notes for Home: Your child paraphrased several paragraphs. *Home Activity:* With your child, find a favorite part of a book, no more than a page or two. Read the passage. Ask your child to tell you what happens in his or her own words.

Name_____

1.	Ⓐ	Ⓑ	Ⓒ	Ⓓ
2.	Ⓕ	Ⓖ	Ⓗ	Ⓙ
3.	Ⓐ	Ⓑ	Ⓒ	Ⓓ
4.	Ⓕ	Ⓖ	Ⓗ	Ⓙ
5.	Ⓐ	Ⓑ	Ⓒ	Ⓓ
6.	Ⓕ	Ⓖ	Ⓗ	Ⓙ
7.	Ⓐ	Ⓑ	Ⓒ	Ⓓ
8.	Ⓕ	Ⓖ	Ⓗ	Ⓙ
9.	Ⓐ	Ⓑ	Ⓒ	Ⓓ
10.	Ⓕ	Ⓖ	Ⓗ	Ⓙ
11.	Ⓐ	Ⓑ	Ⓒ	Ⓓ
12.	Ⓕ	Ⓖ	Ⓗ	Ⓙ
13.	Ⓐ	Ⓑ	Ⓒ	Ⓓ
14.	Ⓕ	Ⓖ	Ⓗ	Ⓙ
15.	Ⓐ	Ⓑ	Ⓒ	Ⓓ

Selection Test

Directions: Choose the best answer to each item. Mark the letter for the answer you have chosen.

Part 1: Vocabulary

Find the answer choice that means about the same as the underlined word in each sentence.

1. The ropes were <u>tangled</u>.
   - A. tied in a bow
   - B. cut by something sharp
   - C. worn along the edge
   - D. twisted in a confused mass

2. The cousins said their <u>farewells</u>.
   - F. good-byes
   - G. prayers
   - H. names
   - J. speeches

3. Dad <u>suggested</u> a new plan.
   - A. refused to allow
   - B. got ready
   - C. put forward the idea
   - D. forced to do

4. Ben <u>flung</u> his cards on the table.
   - F. dropped
   - G. set
   - H. matched
   - J. threw

5. Cassie's sister is <u>vain</u>.
   - A. having too much pride
   - B. showing feelings freely
   - C. hard to understand
   - D. having good manners

6. Someone stole our <u>uniforms</u>.
   - F. things that bring good luck
   - G. clothes worn by members of a group
   - H. small copies of something
   - J. directions for doing something

Part 2: Comprehension

Use what you know about the story to answer each item.

7. Which birds on the ranch had been to Mexico City before?
   - A. the chickens
   - B. the ducks
   - C. the swallows
   - D. the turkeys

8. Half-Chicken was an unusual chick because he—
   - F. had only one wing, one leg, and one eye.
   - G. was born thirteenth.
   - H. was the last chick born.
   - J. wanted to leave the ranch.

GO ON

9. Because of the attention he got, Half-Chicken became very—
   A. shy.
   B. worried.
   C. spoiled.
   D. vain.

10. Half-Chicken left his home because he wanted to—
   F. be a weather vane.
   G. see the court of the viceroy.
   H. meet the wind.
   J. do good deeds.

11. What is another way to say, "I have no time to lose"?
   A. "I'm in a hurry."
   B. "I forgot my watch."
   C. "I have plenty of time."
   D. "I've lost track of time."

12. When Half-Chicken presented himself at the kitchen door of the palace, he—
   F. hoped to be invited in to dinner.
   G. gave the cook a chicken he had brought with him.
   H. didn't realize he was about to become dinner.
   J. was surprised to see his friends were there.

13. What is another way of saying, "This chicken has been more trouble than he's worth"?
   A. "This chicken is too wild to be used in soup."
   B. "This chicken is not worth all the work I've done trying to cook him."
   C. "Now I know why I didn't have to pay for this chicken."
   D. "The trouble is that everything tastes like chicken."

14. What lesson can be learned from this story?
   F. Good things come to those who wait.
   G. People should stay home instead of traveling to see the world.
   H. A bird in the hand is worth two in the bush.
   J. It's good to help others because someday you might need their help.

15. The author was probably trying to be funny when she wrote about a "vain" rooster that—
   A. talked to the wind.
   B. became a weather vane.
   C. was flung out the window.
   D. spoke to the palace guards.

STOP

Predicting

Directions: Read the story. Then read each question about the story. Choose the best answer to each question. Mark the letter for the answer you have chosen.

What Will the Weather Be?

Miriam and her family were on a camping trip. Miriam had just felt a few drops of rain.

"Are you sure that was rain?" Miriam's mother asked. She pointed to the nearby lake, where Miriam's brother was swimming. "Maybe Josh splashed you."

Miriam shook her head. "Look at our campfire," she said. The wind made the flames flicker weakly. "I think that wind means a storm," said Miriam.

Miriam's father looked up at the sky. Overhead, the clouds were dark gray. But way over in the west, the sky was blue and clear. "Maybe the rain clouds will blow over," he said.

Miriam shook her head again. "No," she said. "The wind is blowing in the wrong direction." Then she heard thunder.

1. Based on what you've read, what kind of weather do you predict?
   A. a hurricane
   B. a rainstorm
   C. bright blue skies
   D. a few drops of rain

2. What is the first clue that helps you make your prediction?
   F. Miriam gets splashed by her brother.
   G. Miriam puts out the campfire.
   H. Miriam sees dark gray clouds.
   J. Miriam feels a few raindrops.

3. What is the second clue that helps you make your prediction?
   A. The campfire flickers.
   B. The wind blows leaves into the fire.
   C. Josh splashes Miriam.
   D. The rain starts.

4. Which clue might lead you to predict *good* weather?
   F. The wind is blowing.
   G. Part of the sky is blue.
   H. Dark gray clouds are overhead.
   J. The air is warm.

5. Which clue would lead you to change your "good-weather" prediction?
   A. The wind has died down.
   B. The fire goes out.
   C. Miriam hears thunder.
   D. Josh gets out of the lake.

Notes for Home: Your child made predictions about a story and identified the clues used to make the predictions. ***Home Activity:*** As you complete a task, such as preparing a meal, ask your child to predict what you will do next. Then ask how your child came up with that prediction.

Word Study: Inflected Forms with –es

Directions: Add **-es** to base words ending in **sh, ch, s, ss,** and **x.** Read the paragraph below. Look for words where **-es** has been added. Circle each word and write it on the line.

A mother bird perches on her nest, until one day, a baby bird hatches. A strong wind brushes through the trees. Out falls the baby bird! It passes right through the leafy greenery to the ground. A cat nearby reaches for the baby bird.

"Please don't hurt my baby!" says the mother.

"Why not?" asks the cat.

The mother thinks, then says, "Because one day I will do you a favor."

So the cat lets the baby bird go. A dog sitting nearby watches the cat and catches it. The mother bird sees what has happened. She swoops down and sits on the dog's nose, causing the dog to sneeze and drop the cat. And the cat never bothered another bird again.

1. _____

2. _____

3. _____

4. _____

5. _____

6. _____

7. _____

Directions: Add **-es** to each base word make a new word. Write the new word on the line.

8. fetch _____

9. wash _____

10. wish _____

11. match _____

12. toss _____

13. relax _____

14. teach _____

15. confess _____

Notes for Home: Your child added *-es* to words such as *reach (reaches)* and *pass (passes)*. **Home Activity:** Read a short story with your child. Take turns writing down words you find that end with *-es.*

Thesaurus

A **thesaurus** is a kind of dictionary that contains antonyms, synonyms, and other related words. Like a dictionary, the words are listed alphabetically. You can look up words in a thesaurus to better understand what you read and to find new ways of saying something.

Suppose you wanted to find a new word to replace *peaceful* in the following sentence: *News of the strange Half-Chicken spread quickly to the peaceful cows, grazing with their calves, the fierce bulls, and the swift horses.* First you look up *peaceful* in the index, and then find the entry.

> **peaceful** *(adjective)*
>   *Synonyms:* nonviolent, calm, peaceable
>   *Cross-reference:* cool, unruffled, steady
>   *Antonyms:* disturbed, perturbed, upset

Here is what each part of the entry tells you:

- Part of speech—how a word is used
  Peaceful is an adjective. It is a word that describes nouns.

- Synonyms—words that have the same or similar meanings
  Peaceful means the same or nearly the same as *nonviolent, calm, peaceable.*

- Cross-reference—words that are related to the word you looked up
  You can look up *cool* in the thesaurus for more words with meanings similar to *peaceful.*

- Antonyms—words that have opposite meanings
  Disturbed, perturbed, and *upset* are opposite to *peaceful.*

Directions: The thesaurus entries below give you information about two more words in the sentence on the previous page about Half-Chicken. Use these entries to answer the questions that follow.

---

spread *(verb)*
    Synonyms: circulate, distribute
    Cross-reference: broadcast,
       communicate, pass (on),
       transmit, scatter, sow, peddle
    Antonyms: hold (in), contain

swift *(adjective)*
    Synonyms: fast, quick, rapid,
       snappy, speedy
    Cross-reference: sudden,
       double-quick
    Antonyms: sluggish

---

1. What word is opposite in meaning to *swift?* _____

2. What part of speech is *spread?* _____

3. What part of speech is *swift?* _____

4. What words are synonyms for *spread?* _____

5. Which related words could you look up to find more words similar in meaning to *swift?*

_____

6. Name one antonym for *spread.* _____

7. Which entry word has *pass (on)* as a related word? _____

8. Which entry word is similar in meaning to *speedy?* _____

9. Rewrite the sentence about Half-Chicken. Replace at least one word in the sentence. Use one of the three thesaurus entries shown.

_____

_____

10. Why would a thesaurus be helpful to writers? _____

_____

Notes for Home: Your child used thesaurus entries to locate synonyms, antonyms, and related words. ***Home Activity:*** If you have a thesaurus, have your child find a synonym for *fierce.* Or, ask your child to tell you what synonyms and antonyms are.

Compare and Contrast

- To **compare** is to tell how two or more things are alike. To **contrast** is to tell how two or more things are different.
- Clue words such as *like* or *as* show comparisons. Clue words such as *but, instead,* and *unlike* show contrasts.

Directions: Reread what happens in *Blame It on the Wolf* when the Wolf questions the three little pigs. Then, follow the instructions below.

WOLF: What do you think I said outside your brick house? On the day in question?
IGGIE: I thought you said, "I'll huff and I'll puff and blow you into another galaxy!"
SQUIGGY: I thought he said, "My hands are rough. Can I borrow some moisturizing lotion?"
MOE: I thought he said, "I'll have a BLT on whole wheat—hold the mayo!"

WOLF: So you admit that you really aren't sure what I said. *(to JURY)* I intend to prove that sometimes we don't hear everything clearly. Some people don't pay attention …
JUDGE *(trying to get WOLF'S attention):* Mr. Wolf …
WOLF *(continuing without hearing the JUDGE):* Some people hear only what they want to hear …

1. What is one way in which the pigs' answers are different?

_____

2. What is one way in which Squiggy's and Moe's answers are alike?

_____

3. How is Wolf's opinion different from Iggie's opinion?

_____

4. In what way does the wolf in the courtroom act like the pigs at their house?

_____

5. On a separate sheet of paper, compare and contrast the wolf in this story to the wolf in other stories you know, such as "The Three Little Pigs" and "Little Red Riding Hood."

Notes for Home: Your child compared and contrasted characters in stories to show how they are alike and different. **_Home Activity:_** Find a favorite story. Ask your child how two of the characters in it are alike, and how they are different.

1.	Ⓐ	Ⓑ	Ⓒ	Ⓓ
2.	Ⓕ	Ⓖ	Ⓗ	Ⓙ
3.	Ⓐ	Ⓑ	Ⓒ	Ⓓ
4.	Ⓕ	Ⓖ	Ⓗ	Ⓙ
5.	Ⓐ	Ⓑ	Ⓒ	Ⓓ
6.	Ⓕ	Ⓖ	Ⓗ	Ⓙ
7.	Ⓐ	Ⓑ	Ⓒ	Ⓓ
8.	Ⓕ	Ⓖ	Ⓗ	Ⓙ
9.	Ⓐ	Ⓑ	Ⓒ	Ⓓ
10.	Ⓕ	Ⓖ	Ⓗ	Ⓙ
11.	Ⓐ	Ⓑ	Ⓒ	Ⓓ
12.	Ⓕ	Ⓖ	Ⓗ	Ⓙ
13.	Ⓐ	Ⓑ	Ⓒ	Ⓓ
14.	Ⓕ	Ⓖ	Ⓗ	Ⓙ
15.	Ⓐ	Ⓑ	Ⓒ	Ⓓ

Evaluate Reference Sources

There are many sources you can use to find information. You can use books, magazines, encyclopedias, videotapes, audiotapes, CD-ROMs and even the Internet. When you **evaluate reference sources,** you decide which sources are reliable and up-to-date, and which are most useful for your purpose.

Directions: The table of contents can tell you at a glance what kind of information is in a book. Read the table of contents from two books. Use them to answer the questions that follow.

Wolves
Chapter 1 What do wolves look and sound like?
Chapter 2 What do wolves eat?
Chapter 3 Where do wolves live?

Stories About Wolves
Chapter 1 Little Red Riding Hood
Chapter 2 The Boy Who Cried Wolf
Chapter 3 The Three Little Pigs

1. Which book will give you factual information about how wolves live?

_____

2. Which book will have fictional stories about wolves?

_____

3. Suppose you want to write a report about stories that have wolves as main characters. Will *Stories About Wolves* give you useful information? Explain.

_____

_____

_____

4. Suppose you want to write a report about wolves in the wild and how they live. Will *Wolves* give you useful information? Explain.

_____

_____

_____

Name _____

Directions: A copyright page tells when a book was written. Knowing this information can help you evaluate how up-to-date a source is. Read the copyright pages for two books. Use the copyright information to answer the questions that follow.

Wolves
Copyright © 1972 by Animal Press
All rights reserved.
Animal Press, 537 W. 68th St., New York,
   NY 10015
Fifth Edition

Stories About Wolves
Copyright © 1982 by Children's Book
   Publisher
All rights reserved.
Children's Book Publisher, 239 Red Rd.,
   San Diego, CA 98716
First Edition

---

5. In what year was *Wolves* published? _____

6. In what year was *Stories About Wolves* published? _____

7. Which book is the oldest? _____

8. Suppose you were writing about the number of wolves that exist today. Would you need a book about wolves published more recently than *Wolves?* Explain.

   _____

   _____

9. If you were comparing *Blame It on the Wolf* to the story "The Three Little Pigs," would you need a book published more recently than *Stories About Wolves?* Explain.

   _____

   _____

10. Is it important to think about the purpose of your research before evaluating a reference source? Explain.

   _____

   _____

Notes for Home: Your child evaluated reference sources, based on their contents and when they were published. *Home Activity:* Discuss different reference sources available in your home or at the library. Talk about how each source could be used for different kinds of research projects.

Text Structure

- **Text structure** is the way a piece of writing is organized.
- One way to organize writing is to put events in **chronological,** or time, order.

Directions: Reread "Cal Ripken, Jr." Then complete the time line by listing the important events in Cal Ripken, Jr.'s life.

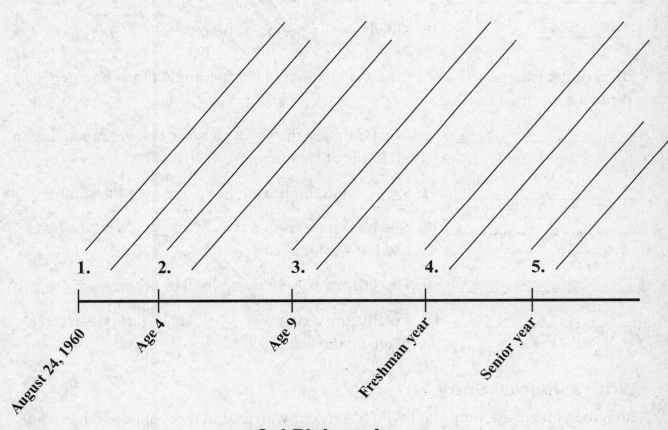

1.   2.   3.   4.   5.

August 24, 1960   Age 4   Age 9   Freshman year   Senior year

Cal Ripken, Jr.

Notes for Home: Your child read a biography and used a time line to show events in the order in which they happened. *Home Activity:* Ask your child to tell the story of his or her life, by telling one memory each from preschool, first grade, second grade, third grade, and so on, in that order.

Name_____

Vocabulary

Directions: Choose the word from the box that best matches each definition. Write the word on the line.

_____	**1.** people who come from a foreign country to live
_____	**2.** caused to believe
_____	**3.** brave
_____	**4.** expert in engineering
_____	**5.** slowly over a period of time

Check the Words You Know

__ convinced
__ courageous
__ engineer
__ gradually
__ immigrants

Directions: Choose the word from the box that the best completes each sentence. Write the word on the line.

_____ **6.** You could see the _____ baseball player practicing in all kinds of weather.

_____ **7.** _____ Marta improved her game over the summer.

_____ **8.** She had come from a family of _____ and they were used to working hard.

_____ **9.** Her brother was studying hard to become an _____.

_____ **10.** Finally, the coach was _____ that Marta deserved a place on the team.

Write a Journal Entry

Imagine you are an immigrant who has recently arrived in this country. On a separate sheet of paper, write a journal entry about your hopes and dreams for your future. Use as many vocabulary words as possible.

Notes for Home: Your child identified and used vocabulary words from *Lou Gehrig: The Luckiest Man. Home Activity:* Ask your child to use each vocabulary word in a sentence. If necessary, show your child how to make up a sentence that includes one of the words.

© Scott Foresman 4

Text Structure

- **Text structure** is the way a piece of writing is organized.
- **Fiction** tells stories of imaginary people and events. They are usually told in chronological, or time, order. **Nonfiction** tells of real people and events or tells information about the real world. Some ways to organize nonfiction are chronological order, cause and effect, problem and solution, or comparison and contrast.

Directions: Reread what happens in *Lou Gehrig: The Luckiest Man* when Lou Gehrig becomes a successful ballplayer. Then answer the questions below.

> After high school Lou Gehrig went to Columbia University. He was on the baseball team there, too, and on April 26, 1923, a scout for the New York Yankees watched him play. Lou hit two long home runs in that game. Soon after that he was signed to play for the Yankees.
>
> The Yankees offered Lou a $1,500 bonus to sign plus a good salary. His family needed the money. Lou quit college and joined the Yankees. Lou's mother was furious. She was convinced that he was ruining his life.
>
> On June 1, 1925, the Yankee manager sent Lou to bat for the shortstop. The next day Lou played in place of first baseman Wally Pipp.

Excerpt from LOU GEHRIG: THE LUCKIEST MAN, copyright © 1997 by David A. Adler, reprinted by permission of Harcourt Brace & Company.

1. What happens before Lou is signed to play for the Yankees?

_____

2. What happens after Lou is offered a $1,500 bonus to sign with the Yankees?

_____

3. What happens on June 1, 1925?

_____

4. How are events in this passage organized?

_____

5. On a separate sheet of paper, tell whether this text is fiction or nonfiction. Then tell how the author organizes his writing. Do you think this is a good way to organize it? Explain.

Notes for Home: Your child looked at the way a text is organized, for example, noticing that events in stories are often told in chronological order. ***Home Activity:*** Ask your child to tell you a story about his or her day, telling about events in the order in which they happened.

Name_____

1.	Ⓐ	Ⓑ	Ⓒ	Ⓓ
2.	Ⓕ	Ⓖ	Ⓗ	Ⓙ
3.	Ⓐ	Ⓑ	Ⓒ	Ⓓ
4.	Ⓕ	Ⓖ	Ⓗ	Ⓙ
5.	Ⓐ	Ⓑ	Ⓒ	Ⓓ
6.	Ⓕ	Ⓖ	Ⓗ	Ⓙ
7.	Ⓐ	Ⓑ	Ⓒ	Ⓓ
8.	Ⓕ	Ⓖ	Ⓗ	Ⓙ
9.	Ⓐ	Ⓑ	Ⓒ	Ⓓ
10.	Ⓕ	Ⓖ	Ⓗ	Ⓙ
11.	Ⓐ	Ⓑ	Ⓒ	Ⓓ
12.	Ⓕ	Ⓖ	Ⓗ	Ⓙ
13.	Ⓐ	Ⓑ	Ⓒ	Ⓓ
14.	Ⓕ	Ⓖ	Ⓗ	Ⓙ
15.	Ⓐ	Ⓑ	Ⓒ	Ⓓ

Selection Test

Directions: Choose the best answer to each item. Mark the letter for the answer you have chosen.

Part 1: Vocabulary

Find the answer choice that means about the same as the underlined word in each sentence.

1. Dana <u>gradually</u> got better.
   A. suddenly
   B. at the end
   C. never
   D. slowly

2. Lee is <u>convinced</u> that he's right.
   F. sure
   G. worried
   H. sorry
   J. aware

3. Are they <u>immigrants</u>?
   A. birds that fly south
   B. persons who come to a foreign country to live
   C. persons who teach others
   D. unusual animals

4. You are very <u>courageous</u>.
   F. clever
   G. popular
   H. special
   J. brave

5. Kyle's mom is an <u>engineer</u>.
   A. one who knows the laws
   B. pilot of an airplane
   C. one who plans and builds things such as bridges
   D. person who plays sports

Part 2: Comprehension

Use what you know about the selection to answer each item.

6. Lou Gehrig was born in—
   F. Baltimore.
   G. Germany.
   H. New York City.
   J. Boston.

7. While Lou Gehrig was in college, he—
   A. became ill.
   B. had to quit school.
   C. gave a speech.
   D. signed to play for the Yankees.

8. Lou's mother was angry when he decided to play baseball because she—
   F. wanted him to be happy.
   G. thought he was ruining his life.
   H. knew he was sick.
   J. needed him to make money.

GO ON

9. Lou Gehrig was known as "Iron Horse" because he—
  A. never missed a game.
  B. hit many home runs.
  C. broke his fingers.
  D. complained often.

10. The text in this selection is organized by—
  F. time order.
  G. causes and effects.
  H. problems and solutions.
  J. how things are alike or different.

11. Which of these events happened first?
  A. Babe Ruth hit 60 home runs.
  B. Gehrig was named MVP.
  C. Babe Ruth hugged Lou Gehrig.
  D. Gehrig got a $1,500 bonus.

12. During the 1938 baseball season, Lou Gehrig's playing got steadily worse because he—
  F. was getting old.
  G. was tired from playing so many games.
  H. stopped believing in himself.
  J. became ill.

13. At the end of his career, Gehrig considered himself lucky because he—
  A. could finally quit baseball.
  B. got a new job right away.
  C. was surrounded by so many caring people.
  D. was voted into the Hall of Fame.

14. The most amazing thing about Lou Gehrig is that he—
  F. was named MVP twice.
  G. never felt sorry for himself.
  H. gave a speech to his fans.
  J. did not know anything was wrong.

15. Which sentence gives an opinion?
  A. Lou's hair was turning gray.
  B. On June 13, 1939, Lou went to the Mayo Clinic.
  C. Lou Gehrig walked to the microphone.
  D. The 1927 Yankees were the best baseball team ever.

STOP

Paraphrasing

Directions: Read the passage. Then read each question about the passage. Choose the best answer to each question. Mark the letter for the answer you have chosen.

Satchel Paige: Baseball Hero

One of the greatest baseball players was the pitcher Satchel Paige.

For most of Paige's life, only white players were allowed in the Major Leagues. So Paige, who was African American, played in the Negro Leagues from the mid-1920s to the mid-1940s.

Paige's fast ball was legendary. Sometimes white players arranged to play against him. He pitched against the famous pitcher Dizzy Dean—and won.

In 1947, Jackie Robinson became the first African American to play in the Major Leagues. In 1948, Paige also joined the Major Leagues.

By then he was in his mid-forties—old for a ballplayer. But he still led his team to the top of the American League. Four years later, he was chosen as an American League All Star.

1. Which statement best paraphrases the first two paragraphs?
   A. Paige played ball for 20 years.
   B. Paige was a great ballplayer.
   C. Paige, a star player, was in the Negro Leagues for 20 years.
   D. Paige was one of the greatest baseball players ever.

2. Which statement does **not** paraphrase the third paragraph?
   F. Paige played in the Majors.
   G. Paige played against great white players.
   H. Paige was a legend in baseball.
   J. Paige attracted great competition.

3. Which phrase best completes this paraphrase of the fourth paragraph? Robinson and Paige both
   A. were stars.
   B. joined the Major Leagues.
   C. were African American.
   D. were great players.

4. Which statement best paraphrases the last paragraph?
   F. Paige still pitched at forty.
   G. Paige was not a young player.
   H. Despite his age, Paige led his team to the top.
   J. Paige was often tired.

5. Which detail does **not** belong in a paraphrase of the last paragraph?
   A. Paige was in his mid-forties.
   B. Robinson joined the Major Leagues.
   C. Paige led his team to the top.
   D. Paige won honors playing.

Notes for Home: Your child paraphrased—restated in his or her own words—a nonfiction passage. *Home Activity:* Tell your child a story about a family member. Then ask your child to retell the story in his or her own words. The paraphrase should keep the story's important ideas.

Word Study: Possessives

Directions: Possessive nouns are words that show ownership. Rewrite each phrase below to show possession. For example, **the scores that the players have** can be written as **the players' scores.** Write the new phrase on the line.

_____ **1.** the ball field that the school has

_____ **2.** the dream that Lou has

_____ **3.** the buildings that cities have

_____ **4.** the rules that schools have

Directions: Read the paragraph below. Several words have apostrophes, but they are not all possessive nouns. Circle each possessive noun. Write the word on the line.

Heroes and heroines in the world of sports make wonderful characters for stories. In such stories, the athletes' goal is usually to overcome an obstacle. For example, they're trying to get along with their teammates. Or a fan's rudeness makes them feel that they'd rather be doing something else. The league's rules might make it impossible for the player to try new things. It's as if the player's own skills aren't good enough for others to believe in. But true athletes are not stopped by other people's fears. Over time, everyone's learned that a strong will and an athlete's dream turn winning into a reality.

5. _____

6. _____

7. _____

8. _____

9. _____

10. _____

Notes for Home: Your child identified possessive nouns, such as *Chris's* and *players'*. **Home Activity:** Read a newspaper article with your child. Together, look for words that have apostrophes. Ask your child to decide whether or not these words show possession.

Name _____

Technology: Order Form

An **order form** is a chart with spaces that need to be filled with specific information. You can use an order form to purchase merchandise from catalogs or to order publications, such as pamphlets, magazines, or newspapers. It is important to follow directions on order forms so that you get what you want.

Print sources, such as catalogs, have order forms that you complete by hand. Electronic sources, such as the Internet, also have order forms. Many companies have Web sites with electronic catalogs. You order items from these catalogs by clicking on pictures or descriptions. The items are automatically listed on an order form and totals are calculated for you. It is important to be careful when using online catalogs and order forms. You may accidentally click on an item you do not want.

Directions: Review these collectors' items available for sale on a baseball Web site. Use the information to answer the questions that follow.

Name _____

1. Mr. Jonas wants to order a 1927 Yankees Baseball Cap. His order form is below. What mistake did he make?

_____

2. Draw a line through the information that Mr. Jonas mistakenly used in the order form above. Write in the item Mr. Jonas meant to order in the row underneath. Add to the order form the Unit Price, Quantity, and Total for this item.

3. Mr. Jonas wants to add to his order. He wants two Lou Gehrig Baseball Cards. Enter this item in the order form.

4. Find the grand total of Mr. Jonas' order. Write it in the order form.

5. How is ordering electronically different from using a printed order form?

_____

_____

_____

Item	Unit Price	Quantity	Total
1927 Yankees Baseball Bat	$72.97	1	$72.97
		Grand Total	

Notes for Home: Your child completed an order form. *Home Activity:* Have your child complete an order form from a catalog. Have him or her select several items. Challenge your child to make the grand total as close to $50 as possible.

Summarizing

- A **summary** is a short statement, no more than a few sentences, that tells the main idea of a selection.
- A **summary of an article** should tell the main idea, leaving out unnecessary details.

Directions: Reread "Korean Food." Then complete the web. Write a sentence summarizing the main idea for each topic given.

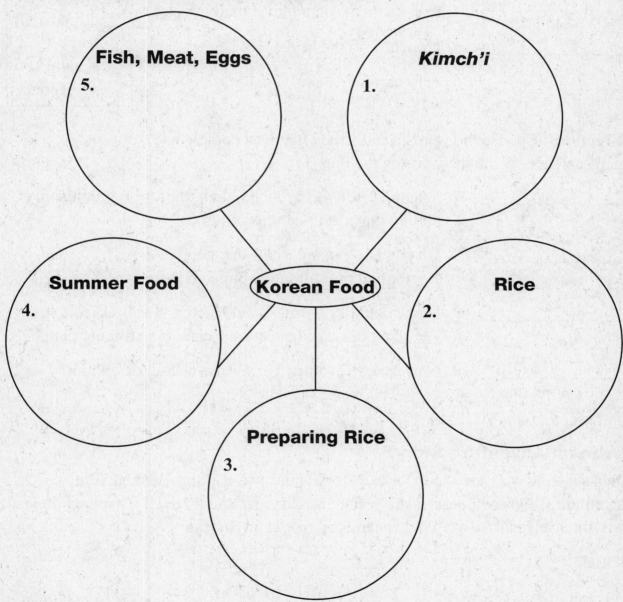

Fish, Meat, Eggs
5.

Kimch'i
1.

Summer Food
4.

Korean Food

Rice
2.

Preparing Rice
3.

Notes for Home: Your child read and summarized the main ideas in an article. **Home Activity:** Ask your child to identify a favorite story, movie, or television episode. Ask your child to summarize its events in no more than a few sentences.

Vocabulary

Directions: Choose the word from the box that best matches each definition. Write the word on the line.

_____ **1.** singing in one tone

_____ **2.** believed to be guilty without proof

_____ **3.** head of a school

_____ **4.** make a thing seem like something else

_____ **5.** crouched on the heels

_____ **6.** very careful

Directions: Choose the word from the box that best completes each sentence. Write the word on the line.

_____ **7.** When Hector was little, he liked to do _____ things like sliding down stairs on his tummy.

_____ **8.** He played so many tricks that people once _____ that Hector had put salt in the punch bowl!

_____ **9.** "How could I do that?" said Hector. "I was asked to _____ a poem while everyone else was drinking punch."

_____ **10.** Now that he is older, Hector has become a lot more _____.

Write an Adventure Story

On a separate sheet of paper, write a story about two children who have an adventure. You might describe how they face danger and then tell what they do to save themselves. Use as many vocabulary words as you can.

Notes for Home: Your child identified and used vocabulary words from "The Disguise."
Home Activity: Play a sentence game with your child. Taking turns, use a vocabulary word in a sentence. The other person has to then use the same word in a different sentence.

Name _____

Summarizing

- A **summary** is a short statement that tells the main ideas of a selection.
- A **story summary** should tell the goals of the characters, how they try to reach them, and whether they reach them. A **summary of an article** should tell the main idea, leaving out unnecessary details.

Directions: Reread what happens in "The Disguise" when Imduk and her mother move to their new home. Then follow the instructions below.

Mother's work-worn hands smoothed the fabric of her black skirt as it lay on the floor. Quickly she began cutting it.

We were in our new home, a single room, in the village of Dukdong. We had planned to live with Mother's brother, but they had quarreled.

He said Mother's idea to educate me was ridiculous. A girl couldn't learn! Where did she get such wild ideas from? No one in their family had such crazy notions!

Stubbornly, Mother clung to her plans and decided to make her own home. This decision took tremendous courage. I knew of no other woman who lived without at least one male relative in her home. By doing this, she was breaking yet another rule of our culture.

From THE GIRL-SON by Anne E. Neuberger. Copyright 1995 by Carolrhoda Books, Inc. Used by permission of the publisher. All rights reserved.

1. What is Mother's goal?

_____

2. Does Mother's brother help her reach that goal?

_____

3. Why did Mother's decision to make her own home take great courage?

_____

4. Write a summary of this passage.

_____

_____

5. Write a summary of "The Disguise" on a separate sheet of paper.

Notes for Home: Your child summarized a story. *Home Activity:* Reread a familiar story with your child. Ask him or her to summarize it for you. Remind your child to think of the main characters, what they want, and how they try to get it.

1.	Ⓐ	Ⓑ	Ⓒ	Ⓓ
2.	Ⓕ	Ⓖ	Ⓗ	Ⓙ
3.	Ⓐ	Ⓑ	Ⓒ	Ⓓ
4.	Ⓕ	Ⓖ	Ⓗ	Ⓙ
5.	Ⓐ	Ⓑ	Ⓒ	Ⓓ
6.	Ⓕ	Ⓖ	Ⓗ	Ⓙ
7.	Ⓐ	Ⓑ	Ⓒ	Ⓓ
8.	Ⓕ	Ⓖ	Ⓗ	Ⓙ
9.	Ⓐ	Ⓑ	Ⓒ	Ⓓ
10.	Ⓕ	Ⓖ	Ⓗ	Ⓙ
11.	Ⓐ	Ⓑ	Ⓒ	Ⓓ
12.	Ⓕ	Ⓖ	Ⓗ	Ⓙ
13.	Ⓐ	Ⓑ	Ⓒ	Ⓓ
14.	Ⓕ	Ⓖ	Ⓗ	Ⓙ
15.	Ⓐ	Ⓑ	Ⓒ	Ⓓ

Selection Test

Directions: Choose the best answer to each item. Mark the letter for the answer you have chosen.

Part 1: Vocabulary

Find the answer choice that means about the same as the underlined word in each sentence.

1. You must <u>disguise</u> yourself.
   A. bring shame upon
   B. become pretty
   C. save from harm
   D. dress to look like someone else

2. Who is the <u>principal</u>?
   F. person who studies
   G. the head of a school
   H. person who swims
   J. member of the police

3. People say I'm too <u>cautious</u>.
   A. polite
   B. very careful
   C. nervous
   D. very smart

4. Everyone <u>suspected</u> that he would be last.
   F. thought it likely
   G. feared
   H. argued
   J. thought well of

5. That sounds <u>dangerous</u>.
   A. comfortable
   B. unusual
   C. unsafe
   D. difficult

6. Can you <u>recite</u> a poem?
   F. explain the meaning of
   G. write over and over
   H. repeat from memory
   J. read from a book

7. The boys were <u>chanting</u>.
   A. singing in one tone
   B. running and shouting playfully
   C. fighting one another
   D. speaking with too much pride

8. Nadine <u>squatted</u> by the fire.
   F. got down on one's knees
   G. fell asleep standing up
   H. lay down
   J. crouched on one's heels

GO ON

Part 2: Comprehension

Use what you know about the story to answer each item.

9. An old man came to Imduk's home to—
   A. make a pink shirt for her.
   B. teach her the Korean alphabet.
   C. show her Chinese characters.
   D. see if she could paint.

10. Imduk's mother decided to move to Dukdong because—
   F. a relative ran a school there.
   G. everyone in their town knew that Imduk was a girl.
   H. there were no teachers nearby.
   J. Dukdong was in China.

11. How were Imduk and the Chinese girl in Mother's story alike?
   A. Both fell in love.
   B. Both liked to swim.
   C. Both knew the alphabet.
   D. Both dressed as boys.

12. Imduk's mother believed that—
   F. Imduk would succeed in school.
   G. girls could not learn.
   H. her husband would return.
   J. going to school was silly.

13. Which sentence best summarizes what happens in this story?
   A. A girl pretended to be a soldier in the army.
   B. Imduk dressed herself as a boy so she could go to school.
   C. Boys in the school wore black ribbons in their hair.
   D. Imduk's mother would not let her swim with the boys.

14. Imduk's mother is the kind of person who—
   F. likes to make people angry.
   G. does not value education.
   H. does what she thinks is right.
   J. will never be happy.

15. Which sentence from the story includes a generalization that is **not** true?
   A. "Most people did not think a girl could be taught to read."
   B. "She seemed deep in thought as she wove and cooked."
   C. "She longed to lead an exciting life."
   D. "I have thought of a way for you to get an education."

STOP

Predicting

Directions: Read the story. Then read each question about the story. Choose the best answer to each question. Mark the letter for the answer you have chosen.

In a New Country

Marc was with his family in Paris, France! Marc could hardly wait to get out and see the sights.

Marc's parents were resting in the next room. But Marc was too excited to rest.

Suddenly, there was a knock on the hotel room door. A voice said something in French. Marc didn't know what to do.

Then Marc remembered that his parents had ordered breakfast. His mother had said that breakfast was brought right to your room.

Marc went to get his parents, and they opened the door. A waiter came in with a tray with three cups of a creamy, brown liquid and a covered dish.

1. Which clues helped you predict who was at the door?
   A. Marc hears a knock.
   B. Marc's mother ordered breakfast at the hotel.
   C. Marc is in Paris, France.
   D. Marc's parents are next door.

2. Which of the following is most likely to be in the three cups?
   F. soup
   G. orange juice
   H. coffee or hot chocolate
   J. gravy

3. Which of the following is most likely to be under the covered dish?
   A. roast beef
   B. ham sandwiches
   C. ice cream
   D. rolls and butter

4. What do you predict Marc will do after breakfast?
   F. He will take a nap.
   G. He will make a phone call.
   H. He will go sightseeing.
   J. He will read a book.

5. Which clue helped you predict what Marc will do next?
   A. Marc hears a knock at the door.
   B. Marc and his parents are staying in a hotel.
   C. Marc hears some French.
   D. Marc can hardly wait to get out and see the sights.

Notes for Home: Your child made predictions based on information read in a story. *Home Activity:* Play a "prediction game" with your child. Take turns giving each other clues and making predictions. For example: *I'm at the gas station. What do you predict I'll do next?* (*buy gas*)

Word Study: Suffixes

Directions: Suffixes are letters we add to the end of base words. Some suffixes are **-ful, -ly, -ion, -ous, -less, -ness,** and **-ment.** Read the journal entry below. Find each word that has one of these suffixes and write it on a line.

Dear Diary,

Today was a wonderful day! I wanted to see if a girl could join the boys' basketball team. I know it may not be a wise decision. It might even be dangerous. Some might even say my case was hopeless. But I had to try, even if it was only to make a statement about girls being good sports. Quickly I donned my disguise. I walked uneasily onto the court. I was careful to make sure no one recognized me. As the game started, I knew that the team was about to get an education it would never forget. In all fairness, it's a lesson they need to learn.

1. _____

2. _____

3. _____

4. _____

5. _____

6. _____

7. _____

8. _____

9. _____

10. _____

Directions: Each word below has a base word and one or two suffixes. Write the base word in the first column. Then write the suffix or suffixes in the second column.

	Base Word	Suffix or Suffixes
11. beautifully	_____	_____
12. pollution	_____	_____
13. carelessly	_____	_____
14. encouragement	_____	_____
15. joyously	_____	_____

Notes for Home: Your child identified suffixes, and added them to the ends of words. ***Home Activity:*** Play a game with your child. Write a word like *encourage.* Then write some suffixes, like *-ly, -ous,* and *-ment.* Have your child choose a suffix to make a new word.

© Scott Foresman 4

Alphabetical Order

The words in glossaries and indexes are organized in **alphabetical order** to make them easier to find. To find an entry in an alphabetical list, start by looking for the first letter of the word you wish to find. If there are multiple entries with the same first letter, look for the second letter. If there are multiple entries with the same first and second letters, look for the third letter, and so on.

You can use alphabetical order to get information from a telephone book, a dictionary, and an encyclopedia too. You'll also find fiction books in a library organized on shelves by alphabetical order using the authors' last names.

Directions: Use this index listing from an almanac to find each topic listed below. Write the page number or numbers where information about this topic can be found.

A

Abbreviations, 112
Acid rain, 44
Afghanistan, 36
Africa
   Facts, 98
   History, 104, 216–217
   Map, 398
Alabama, 235
Alaska, 389
Angola, 67
Animals, 46–50
   Classifying, 46
   Endangered species, 87
   Fastest and largest, 50
Antarctica, 77
Antigua, 32–33
Arctic Ocean, 80
Argentina, 36–37
   Map, 398
Arizona, 135
Arkansas, 136
Armenia, 38–39
Art, 79–83

1. Alabama _____

2. Arizona _____

3. Antigua _____

4. a map of Africa _____

5. endangered animals _____

6. largest animal _____

7. African history _____

8. Arctic Ocean _____

9. map of Argentina _____

10. snakes _____

Directions: Some of the words from the glossary below are missing. Choose the best word from the box to complete each glossary entry. Hint: The list should be in alphabetical order.

principal	chanting	disguise
dangerous	cautious	recite

11. _____, very careful

   chanting, singing in one tone

12. _____, likely to cause harm

13. _____, make it seem like something else

   principal, head of a school

14. _____, say over; repeat

15. Why is alphabetical order a useful way to organize information? Give an example
    of a reference source that uses alphabetical order to support your answer.

   _____

   _____

   _____

   _____

   _____

   _____

   _____

   _____

Notes for Home: Your child learned ways to use alphabetical order. *Home Activity:* Take turns challenging each other to find names in a phone book or topics in an encyclopedia. Or, have your child list favorite television shows in alphabetical order.

Plot

- Stories have **plot,** or a series of events that center on a problem, or conflict.
- A conflict can be a problem between two people or groups, between a person and nature, or within a character.
- The climax is the place where the action builds, and the conflict must be faced. The resolution is where the conflict is solved.

Directions: Reread "One Particular Small, Smart Boy." Then complete the plot map. Use the questions to help you describe the conflict, events that lead to the climax, and how the conflict is resolved.

What does the boy
do last to confront
the problem?

4. _____

What does the   _____
boy do next?   _____

3. _____   What finally
                                               happens?

What does the   _____
boy do first to   _____   5. _____
solve the problem?   _____

2. _____   _____
   _____

What is the
problem?

1. _____

   _____

   _____

Notes for Home: Your child read a story and described its plot. *Home Activity:* Ask your child to tell you the plot of a favorite story. Make sure your child tells you the main problem, the events that lead up to the problem being solved, and the way the problem is solved.

Vocabulary

Directions: Choose the word from the box that best completes each sentence. Write the word on the line to the left.

	Check the Words You Know
	__ considering
	__ definitely
	__ diamond
	__ grounders
	__ reminder
	__ stroke
	__ taunted

_____ 1. Omar is _____ the best ball player I know.

_____ 2. He can easily scoop up those hard-to-catch _____ that batters often hit.

_____ 3. As soon as the ball hits his glove, Omar throws it to his teammates inside the baseball _____.

_____ 4. Last year Omar's grandmother had a sudden _____, and he quit baseball to help take care of her.

_____ 5. Some of the other kids _____ Omar for being a quitter.

_____ 6. _____ how mean these kids were being, I think Omar kept his temper well.

_____ 7. "Whenever I start to get mad," he said, "I think of my grandmother. She is a good _____ to stay calm."

Directions: Cross out the word or words that do not belong in each group.

8. taunted   teased   cheered   insulted
9. definitely   certainly   surely   possibly
10. considering   forgetting   thinking about   keeping in mind

Write a Thank-You Note

On a separate page, write a letter to a relative saying "thank you" for something special he or she did for you. Use as many vocabulary words as you can.

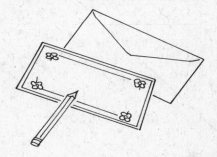

Notes for Home: Your child identified and used vocabulary words from *Keepers*. **Home Activity:** Play a definition game with your child. You say a vocabulary word, and he or she tells you its definition. For extra fun, have your child give a definition and you guess the word.

Plot

• A story's **plot** is the important parts of the story. The parts of a plot are the conflict, or problem, the rising action, the climax, and the resolution, or outcome.

Directions: Reread what happens in *Keepers* when Little Dolly tells her grandson, Kenyon, what a Keeper is. Then answer the questions below.

> "The Keeper holds onto the past until she can pass it on to the next." Little Dolly squinched her dark brown eyes. "Don't know who I'll hand my tales to, though." Her large fingers plucked at the sleeve of her blouse.
> Kenyon stopped the swing and he knelt beside her. "Little Dolly, I'll be the Keeper, I love your stories."
> Her eyes looked deep into his, searching.
> "Lord, honey, that's nice, but you a boy. I got to find me a girl Keeper. You can't be a Keeper if you a boy."
>
> Text copyright © Jeri Hanel Watts. Excerpt from KEEPERS. Reprinted by arrangement with Lee & Low Books, Inc.

1. What problem does Little Dolly have?

_____

2. What does Kenyon want?

_____

3. Why can't he get what he wants?

_____

_____

4. What might Kenyon do to get what he wants?

_____

_____

5. On a separate sheet of paper, describe the plot of *Keepers*. Tell what problem is at the center of the story, and how this problem is faced during the climax of the story and resolved.

Notes for Home: Your child identified the plot—the important parts of a story. *Home Activity:* Reread a favorite story with your child. Ask him or her to tell you the plot, including the main problem, or conflict, in the story and how this problem is resolved by the end.

Name_____

1.	Ⓐ	Ⓑ	Ⓒ	Ⓓ
2.	Ⓕ	Ⓖ	Ⓗ	Ⓙ
3.	Ⓐ	Ⓑ	Ⓒ	Ⓓ
4.	Ⓕ	Ⓖ	Ⓗ	Ⓙ
5.	Ⓐ	Ⓑ	Ⓒ	Ⓓ
6.	Ⓕ	Ⓖ	Ⓗ	Ⓙ
7.	Ⓐ	Ⓑ	Ⓒ	Ⓓ
8.	Ⓕ	Ⓖ	Ⓗ	Ⓙ
9.	Ⓐ	Ⓑ	Ⓒ	Ⓓ
10.	Ⓕ	Ⓖ	Ⓗ	Ⓙ
11.	Ⓐ	Ⓑ	Ⓒ	Ⓓ
12.	Ⓕ	Ⓖ	Ⓗ	Ⓙ
13.	Ⓐ	Ⓑ	Ⓒ	Ⓓ
14.	Ⓕ	Ⓖ	Ⓗ	Ⓙ
15.	Ⓐ	Ⓑ	Ⓒ	Ⓓ

Selection Test

Directions: Choose the best answer to each item. Mark the letter for the answer you have chosen.

Part 1: Vocabulary

Find the answer choice that means about the same as the underlined word in each sentence.

1. The team left the <u>diamond</u>.
   A. dugout
   B. baseball field
   C. bus
   D. place where fans sit

2. Marc <u>taunted</u> his brother.
   F. greeted in a friendly way
   G. surprised
   H. teased in a mean way
   J. honored

3. Patti caught some <u>grounders</u>.
   A. baseballs hit along the ground
   B. small animals with bushy tails
   C. birds that cannot fly
   D. balls hit high into the air

4. Today is <u>definitely</u> a good day.
   F. probably
   G. usually
   H. fortunately
   J. certainly

5. Will you need a <u>reminder</u>?
   A. permit to build something
   B. something to help one remember
   C. set of instructions
   D. written statement that money has been received

6. Fiona is <u>considering</u> buying a new coat.
   F. thinking seriously about
   G. trying to keep away from
   H. making a habit of
   J. taking pleasure in

7. Terry's uncle had a <u>stroke</u>.
   A. illness caused by bleeding in the brain
   B. pain in a tooth
   C. long talk about something
   D. time of good luck

Part 2: Comprehension

Use what you know about the story to answer each item.

8. Kenyon's grandmother is a Keeper of—
   F. birthday presents.
   G. homework.
   H. stories and legends.
   J. chocolates.

GO ON

9. Kenyon is not allowed to go out and play baseball until—
   A. he finishes his homework.
   B. he gets a new glove.
   C. his grandmother falls asleep.
   D. his friends call for him.

10. Little Dolly tells Kenyon that he can't be a Keeper because he—
    F. doesn't know enough stories.
    G. is a boy.
    H. plays too much baseball.
    J. can't remember things.

11. What is Kenyon's main conflict?
    A. He can't get his homework done.
    B. He can't hit Mo Davis's fastball.
    C. He doesn't want to take care of his grandmother.
    D. He buys a new glove and has no money left for a present.

12. You can tell that a "wallop-bat day" is a day when—
    F. Kenyon plays baseball.
    G. everything goes well.
    H. Kenyon forgets something.
    J. someone makes a mistake.

13. The climax of the story comes when—
    A. Kenyon goes shopping.
    B. Mrs. Montgomery walks up to the house.
    C. Kenyon gives the book to his grandmother.
    D. Little Dolly gets some chocolates.

14. Mrs. Montgomery and the others come to the house to—
    F. see Kenyon's baseball glove.
    G. surprise Little Dolly with her favorite things.
    H. see what Kenyon gives to his grandmother.
    J. show Kenyon that they know he has made a book.

15. This story shows that—
    A. baseball gloves made of real leather are expensive.
    B. few people live to be ninety.
    C. a birthday should be a big event.
    D. some of the best presents don't cost anything.

Steps in a Process

Directions: Read the passage. Then read each question about the passage. Choose the best answer to each question. Mark the letter for the answer you have chosen.

Making a Family Album

Have you ever thought of making a family album? The first thing to do is to find an album. A nice, big sturdy album is best. Make sure that the album has pages made out of paper, not plastic. It's hard to paste things onto plastic.

The next thing to do is collect family treasures to go in the album. Some treasures you might collect are photographs, tickets or programs from special events, or postcards.

After that, you'll want to organize the treasures. You could give each family member a page or try to put things in chronological order.

Finally, label each treasure and write something about it. Ask family members to help.

1. What is the first step in the process?
   A. putting things in order
   B. talking to the family
   C. finding an album
   D. pasting things onto paper

2. What clue word tells you what the second step is?
   F. second
   G. after
   H. finally
   J. next

3. What is the third step in the process?
   A. organizing the treasures
   B. asking for treasures
   C. collecting treasures
   D. labeling each treasure

4. What clue word or words tells you what the third step is?
   F. after that
   G. could give
   H. organize
   J. chronological order

5. What clue word tells you what the last step is?
   A. finally
   B. after that
   C. next
   D. share

Notes for Home: Your child identified steps in a process that tell the order of steps to be done to complete an action. *Home Activity:* Choose a familiar activity, such as making a sandwich. Have your child tell you four or five steps in the process of that activity. The steps should be told in order.

Word Study: Syllabication

Directions: Syllables are the individual parts of a word that you
hear. For example, when you say the word **syllable,** you hear three
separate parts: **syl • la • ble.** Read the sentences below. Say the
underlined word to yourself. Write the syllables on the lines like this:
syl • la • ble.

_____ **1.** The class was so interested in the story that they
never <u>interrupted</u> the storyteller.

_____ **2.** A good storyteller makes <u>characters</u> come to life.

_____ **3.** <u>Muttering</u> is no way to tell a good story.

_____ **4.** My <u>grandmother</u> is a great storyteller.

_____ **5.** My <u>favorite</u> part of her stories is when the characters
learn a lesson.

Directions: Read the words in the box. Count how many syllables
each word has. Sort the words according to the number of syllables.
Write each word in the correct column.

| neighborhood   letters   dollars   holidays |

Words with Two Syllables

6. _____

7. _____

Words with Three Syllables

8. _____

9. _____

Directions: Read this word and say it to yourself: **apologizing.** Write the number
of syllables in the word, and then write each syllable.

10. Number of syllables: _____   Syllables: _____

Notes for Home: Your child divided longer words into individual syllables. ***Home Activity:***
Read a poem with your child. Select important words from the poem for you and your child to
read and say together. Help your child say each word and count the syllables.

Time Line

A **time line** is a special kind of chart that shows events in the order in which they happened or will happen. The bar of a time line is divided into units of time, such as months, years, or decades. It is labeled with the event.

Directions: Think of ten events that have become often-told family stories about you and your family, such as a camping trip to the Rockies or the birth of a little sister. Describe the events on the lines below. Tell how old you were for each event. Then figure out the year each event took place. Record the month the event took place, if you can.

Family Events	My Age	Year/Month
_____	_____	_____
_____	_____	_____
_____	_____	_____
_____	_____	_____
_____	_____	_____
_____	_____	_____
_____	_____	_____
_____	_____	_____
_____	_____	_____
_____	_____	_____
_____	_____	_____

© Scott Foresman 4

Directions: Use the bar below to make a time line of your family events. First, divide the bar into equal parts to show the number of years your time line will cover. For example, if your events cover a 10-year period, divide the bar into 10 equal parts. Then write the year (and month if you know it) that each event took place above the line. Write a short description of each event below the line. Draw lines connecting the labels to the bar. Make sure that the events and years match and that events are listed in the order in which they happened.

Notes for Home: Your child made a time line of family events. *Home Activity:* Tell your child some of your favorite family stories about special events. Together, make a time line of these events.

© Scott Foresman 4

Summarizing

> • A **summary** gives the main ideas of an article, or it tells what happens in a story.
> • A summary is short, and it doesn't include unimportant details.

Directions: Reread "Stagecoaches Then . . . and Now." Then complete the table. List details that belong with each topic. Then write a sentence summarizing the article.

Topic	Summary
Movie image of stages vs. reality	Movie Image: exciting, almost always ambushed by robbers **1.** Reality:
How stages began	**2.**
How stages got name	**3.**
How stages made money	**4.**

Summary of Article

5. _____

_____

_____

Notes for Home: Your child read an article and summarized its main idea. *Home Activity:* Read an article from a children's magazine or watch a TV documentary with your child. Ask him or her to summarize the main idea.

Vocabulary

Directions: Choose the word from the box that best matches each definition. Write the word on the line.

_____ 1. deep, narrow valleys

_____ 2. a way of sending coded messages
over wires

_____ 3. part of a machine that sets it in
motion

_____ 4. ironworker

_____ 5. blacksmith's shop

_____ 6. reliable

Directions: Read the help wanted ad. Choose the word from the box that best completes each sentence. Write the word on the matching numbered line.

Blacksmith Needed

We need a **7.** _____ person that can be trusted to work hard. The new blacksmith would work in the **8.** _____ with five other workers. You must be willing to travel across two deep **9.** _____ to get to work each day. If interested, please use a **10.** _____ to send your response because we don't have a telephone.

7. _____

8. _____

9. _____

10. _____

Write Dictionary Entries

Make dictionary entries for three of the vocabulary words. Each dictionary entry should have the word, a definition, and a picture. You may wish to look at pictures in a history book or encyclopedia. Pictures make the words easier to understand!

Notes for Home: Your child identified and used new vocabulary words from "Amazing Alice!" *Home Activity:* Work with your child to write a story about hiring a blacksmith to fix something for you.

Summarizing

- A **summary** is a short statement that tells the main idea of a selection, leaving out unimportant details.

Directions: Reread this passage from "Amazing Alice!" Then answer the questions below. Use what you know about summarizing.

> There were only 20 more miles to go until we reached the ferry house at Oakland, where we would board a boat taking us across the wide, blue bay to San Francisco. Time sped by too quickly. We arrived at the Oakland boat dock within an hour after breakfast. Once on the ferry, we set the Maxwell's brakes and raced to the front end of the boat to watch San Francisco bobbing in the water. Great golliwogs! To think that those same Pacific Ocean waves touch the shores of the Chinese Empire!
>
> Our ferry slid out into the bay. Gulls were squawking like New York street vendors. Buoys were clanging. We heard foghorns hoot, though there was no fog. The other passengers seemed very excited to get a look at the Maxwell and us. Who told them I don't know, but everyone knew where we were from and what Alice had done. We did not have a single quiet moment, as every rider wanted to congratulate us.

From COAST TO COAST WITH ALICE by Patricia Rusch Hyatt. Copyright © 1995 by Carolrhoda Books, Inc. Used by permission of the publisher. All rights reserved.

1. Why isn't the following sentence a good example of a summary for the first paragraph? *It was 20 more miles to the ferry house.*

_____

2. Write a summary of the first paragraph.

_____

3. Is the following sentence a good summary of the second paragraph? Explain. *The ferry boat ride was noisy.*

_____

4. What is the main idea of the second paragraph?

_____

5. On a separate sheet of paper, write a summary of "Amazing Alice!"

Notes for Home: Your child used story details to summarize a passage. ***Home Activity:*** Take turns with your child reading short articles from a newspaper or magazine and summarizing them. Decide what is the main idea of each article and what are unimportant details.

1.	Ⓐ	Ⓑ	Ⓒ	Ⓓ
2.	Ⓕ	Ⓖ	Ⓗ	Ⓙ
3.	Ⓐ	Ⓑ	Ⓒ	Ⓓ
4.	Ⓕ	Ⓖ	Ⓗ	Ⓙ
5.	Ⓐ	Ⓑ	Ⓒ	Ⓓ
6.	Ⓕ	Ⓖ	Ⓗ	Ⓙ
7.	Ⓐ	Ⓑ	Ⓒ	Ⓓ
8.	Ⓕ	Ⓖ	Ⓗ	Ⓙ
9.	Ⓐ	Ⓑ	Ⓒ	Ⓓ
10.	Ⓕ	Ⓖ	Ⓗ	Ⓙ
11.	Ⓐ	Ⓑ	Ⓒ	Ⓓ
12.	Ⓕ	Ⓖ	Ⓗ	Ⓙ
13.	Ⓐ	Ⓑ	Ⓒ	Ⓓ
14.	Ⓕ	Ⓖ	Ⓗ	Ⓙ
15.	Ⓐ	Ⓑ	Ⓒ	Ⓓ

Selection Test

Directions: Choose the best answer to each item. Mark the letter for the answer you have chosen.

Part 1: Vocabulary

Find the answer choice that means about the same as the underlined word in each sentence.

1. He will underline{telegraph} his answer.
   A. send a message by wire
   B. look for
   C. watch from a distance
   D. join

2. Joan is a underline{dependable} person.
   F. interesting
   G. able to be counted on
   H. clever
   J. funny or amusing

3. This is the underline{crank}.
   A. sheet of metal
   B. type of map
   C. a narrow bridge
   D. handle on a machine

4. He found a underline{blacksmith}.
   F. ironworker
   G. storyteller
   H. driver
   J. news reporter

5. Tell us about the underline{ravines}.
   A. strong winds
   B. small streams
   C. words of praise
   D. deep, narrow valleys

6. The underline{forge} is open now.
   F. place to cross a river
   G. shelter or station
   H. shop for metal work
   J. place for meetings

Part 2: Comprehension

Use what you know about the selection to answer each item.

7. Alice was the first woman to—
   A. drive across the country.
   B. own a car.
   C. fix cars for a living.
   D. enter a contest.

8. This selection is written as if it were told by—
   F. Alice.
   G. Minna.
   H. Maggie.
   J. Nettie.

GO ON

9. How did Minna feel about Alice?
  A. She was jealous of her.
  B. She thought she was strange.
  C. She admired her.
  D. She thought she was bossy.

10. What did the women learn about the "Blue Book"?
  F. It was easy to use.
  G. Parts of it were out of date.
  H. It had very good maps.
  J. Most of it was about the West.

11. Which sentence best summarizes what happened in Wyoming?
  A. The women walked across a railroad bridge to get a permit to drive across it.
  B. The bridge across the river had been washed away.
  C. A train came along while the women were crossing the trestle bridge.
  D. Alice got a case of "jolt-itis."

12. The entries in this journal tell mostly about—
  F. what Alice was like.
  G. how the women got along.
  H. the challenges of the trip.
  J. how homesick Minna felt.

13. Which sentence best summarizes this selection?
  A. Alice drove over a prairie dog hole and broke an axle.
  B. Alice Ramsey and three other women drove across the United States in 59 days.
  C. Alice and her friends drove all day and stayed in a different hotel every night.
  D. Alice drove the car and told Minna what to write in her journal.

14. Which sentence gives an opinion?
  F. "There were only 20 more miles to go."
  G. "Time sped by too quickly."
  H. "We arrived at the Oakland boat dock."
  J. "Our ferry slid out into the bay."

15. What made Alice an unusual woman for her time?
  A. She was smart.
  B. She had a good friend.
  C. She liked traveling.
  D. She was an expert driver.

Graphic Sources

REVIEW

Directions: Read the passage and look at the bar graph. Then read each question about the passage and the bar graph. Choose the best answer to each question. Mark the letter for the answer you have chosen.

Henry Ford's Car

In 1903, Ford Motor Company sold its first car. But real success came in 1908, with the Model T car.

Then in 1913, Ford's assembly line greatly cut the time it took to make a Model T car. The price also kept coming down. By the mid-1920s, many working people could afford a Model T car and the company's sales soared.

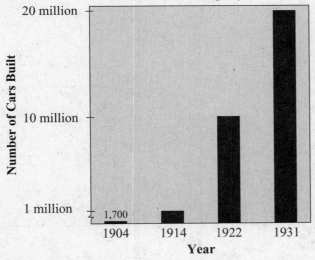

Ford: A Car Company Grows

Number of Cars Built / Year

1. Ford Motor Company built its millionth car in—
   A. 1914.
   B. 1922.
   C 1908.
   D. 1931.

2. About how many cars did Ford build in 1922?
   F. 1,000
   G. 1 million
   H. 10 million
   J. 20 million

3. The price of the Model T car dropped because of—
   A. the assembly line.
   B. the Depression.
   C. cheaper materials.
   D. their bumpy ride.

4. How long after it built its 10 millionth car did Ford build its 20 millionth car?
   F. about 20 years
   G. about 10 years
   H. only one year
   J. 31 years later

5. In what year did the Ford Motor Company build its 30 millionth car?
   A. 1933
   B. 1943
   C. 1922
   D. can't tell from facts given

Notes for Home: Your child read a passage and interpreted a bar graph. *Home Activity:* Look for graphs in the newspaper with your child. Take turns asking one another questions based on information in the graph. Discuss how you used the graph to answer each question.

Word Study: Prefixes

Directions: Letters added to the beginning of words are called **prefixes.** Prefixes can change the meaning of the base word. Add the prefix to each word below to make a new word. Write each new word on the line.

	Prefix		Base Word		New Word
1.	dis	+	obey	=	_____
2.	re	+	paint	=	_____
3.	mis	+	lead	=	_____
4.	un	+	hooked	=	_____
5.	il	+	logical	=	_____

Directions: Read the journal entry below. Look for words with the prefix: **dis-, re, mis-, un-, il-, sub-, en-,** or **in-.** Circle each word and write it on the line.

March 31
My family and I are starting our trip today. We are driving across the country! It's not an uncommon trip, but it's new to me. My parents have always encouraged me to try new things. I watched as familiar sights disappeared. We'd only gone a few hours, when my father misread the map! He could not make an illegal U-turn to head us back in the right direction. But we were not discouraged! We drove to where we could turn around, retraced our steps, and started again. My father is not often incorrect about directions. Maybe we should have a subtitle for this trip— "Our Unpredictable Adventure."

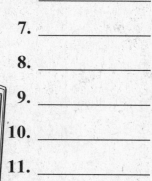

6. _____

7. _____

8. _____

9. _____

10. _____

11. _____

12. _____

13. _____

14. _____

15. _____

Notes for Home: Your child wrote and identified words with prefixes, such as *disappear (dis + appear)*. **Home Activity:** Read a newspaper story with your child. Work together to find words with the prefixes listed above.

Technology: Manual

A **manual** is a written set of directions, usually in the form of a booklet or book, that helps readers understand or use something. To understand a manual, you need to know how to follow directions.

Directions: The *Everyday Spelling* CD-ROM contains lessons, games, and activities that can help you learn to spell. Use this page from the manual to answer the questions on the next page.

The *Everyday Spelling* textbook program consists of weekly spelling lessons, review lessons, and cross-cultural lessons. The lockers ("cubbies" in grades 1 and 2) on this screen represent lessons. Selecting locker 1, for example, lets you use the words from Lesson 1. Move the cursor to a number and click on it to choose the words you will use.

Lockers numbered 1–5, 7–11, 13–17, 19–23, 25–29, and 31–35 will take you to the Classroom area, where you will work with that lesson's spelling words. Every sixth lesson is a review lesson. Lockers numbered 6, 12, 18, 24, 30, and 36 will take you to the Testing Center, where you will work with spelling words in review lessons.

Note: In grade 1 there are no spelling lessons 1–6.

From EVERYDAY SPELLING CD–ROM USER'S GUIDE. Copyright © 1998. Addison-Wesley Educational Publishers Inc.

Name_____

1. What are three different kinds of lessons in the textbook program?

_____

2. What does each locker represent? _____

3. How can you get to the spelling words for Lesson 5? _____

_____

4. Which locker would you click on if you wanted to review spelling words for Lessons 1–5?

_____

5. Clicking on lockers will take you to two different areas to work with spelling words. To what two areas can you go?

_____

6. When you click on locker 22, what will happen? _____

_____

7. When you click on locker 12, what will happen?

_____

8. Which lessons are review lessons? _____

9. Why do you think the manual shows the program's computer screens?

_____

_____

10. Why is it important to know how to follow directions to use a manual?

_____

_____

_____

Notes for Home: Your child read a manual for a CD-ROM program and answered questions about it. *Home Activity:* Find a user's manual for an appliance or a computer program. Look through the manual with your child and discuss the kinds of information that can be found in it.

Visualizing

Directions: Read the story. Then read each question about the story. Choose the best answer to each question. Mark the letter for the answer you have chosen.

Across the Border

July 4, 1976. Pedro was in the car, heading up the west coast. He gazed at the ocean waves crashing against the shore. Just last week, he had been living across the border in Mexico with his aunt. Then his mother had come to take Pedro and his sister, Pilar, to California. They were all going to live in America.

Pedro could hardly sit still. He imagined his new home with the whitewashed walls, the picket fence, and the yard with chickens. He could smell his mother's cooking.

The car headed away from the coast. It climbed through some hills. Then it went down into a small valley.

The sky darkened. Pedro heard a booming noise. To the right he saw brilliant flashes of color sparkle in the night sky. What a way to celebrate his coming to America!

1. In the car, Pedro—
   A. gets carsick.
   B. sees the ocean.
   C. sees Mexico.
   D. spots his new home.

2. When Pedro imagines his new home, he—
   F. wants to return to Mexico.
   G. feels excited.
   H. laughs at his mother.
   J. tells Pilar.

3. The car ride was probably—
   A. uncomfortable.
   B. interesting.
   C. frightening.
   D. boring.

4. Pedro's new home is probably in—
   F. an apartment building.
   G. the city.
   H. a suburban house.
   J. the country.

5. The booming noise Pedro hears and the colorful sparkles of light are—
   A. signs of danger.
   B. signs of a thunderstorm.
   C. fireworks.
   D. especially created for Pedro.

© Scott Foresman 4

Notes for Home: Your child used story details to visualize or imagine what is happening in a story. *Home Activity:* Have your child look carefully at a room, and then give vivid details that would help someone else mentally picture this place.

Phonics: Words with Silent Consonants *kn, gn, wr, mb*

Directions: Read the words below. One consonant in each word is silent. Write the silent consonant on the line.

1. knee _____

2. resigned _____

3. wrote _____

4. comb _____

5. wrap _____

6. numb _____

7. gnarled _____

8. knitted _____

9. wreck _____

10. dumb _____

Directions: Read the words in the box. Cross out the words that do **not** have silent consonants. Use the remaining words to complete the sentences below. Write the words on the lines to the left.

knocking	bit	wrong	calling	incorrect
designs	gnawed	created	knots	butterflies

_____ **11.** Like many Europeans of his time, Jan heard opportunity _____ in America.

_____ **12.** Young Jan followed his dream and came to America, where he _____ clothing for a new store.

_____ **13.** Now Jan's stomach twisted into _____ as he wondered whether the shop would be a success.

_____ **14.** He _____ his lips nervously as he unlocked the door for the first day of business.

_____ **15.** The crowd of eager customers showed Jan that his creative ideas had not been _____.

Notes for Home: Your child identified words with *kn, gn, wr,* and *mb* where one consonant in each pair is silent, like <u>kn</u>ow, si<u>gn</u>, <u>wr</u>ite, and com<u>b</u>. **Home Activity:** Read a newspaper article with your child. Help your child find words that have silent consonants.

© Scott Foresman 4

Graphic Sources

• A **graphic source** is an illustration, a graph, a chart, a map, a diagram, or other visual aid that helps you by showing you what the words say, or by organizing information in a useful way.

Directions: Reread this passage from "The Race for the North Pole" and look at the map. The black arrows show some of Matthew Henson's travels. Then answer the questions below.

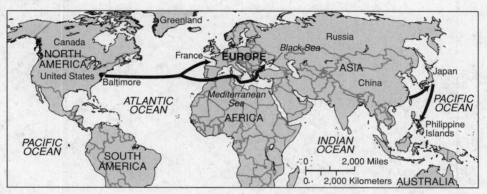

Matthew sailed from China to Japan to the Philippines. He sailed across the Atlantic Ocean to France, Africa, and southern Russia. He even sailed through the Arctic. And all the time, he continued to learn. When Matthew was 19, Captain Childs died and was buried at sea. Heartbroken, Matthew returned to Baltimore.

From ROBERT PEARY & MATTHEW HENSON: THE RACE FOR THE NORTH POLE by Laurie Rozakis.
Copyright © 1994 by Blackbirch Press, Inc. Reprinted by permission.

1. To sail from Japan to the Philippines, Matthew Henson sailed upon which ocean?

_____

2. To which continents did Matthew Henson sail?

_____

3. To go from Africa to southern Russia, which seas may Henson have sailed?

_____

4. Where is Baltimore? _____

5. What information does a map give that helps you to better understand a passage like the one above? Write your answer on a separate sheet of paper.

Notes for Home: Your child read a story and used a map to understand story details better. *Home Activity:* Look at a map with your child (such as a newspaper weather map, a map in an atlas, or a website map). Take turns asking each other questions like the ones above.

1.	Ⓐ	Ⓑ	Ⓒ	Ⓓ
2.	Ⓕ	Ⓖ	Ⓗ	Ⓙ
3.	Ⓐ	Ⓑ	Ⓒ	Ⓓ
4.	Ⓕ	Ⓖ	Ⓗ	Ⓙ
5.	Ⓐ	Ⓑ	Ⓒ	Ⓓ
6.	Ⓕ	Ⓖ	Ⓗ	Ⓙ
7.	Ⓐ	Ⓑ	Ⓒ	Ⓓ
8.	Ⓕ	Ⓖ	Ⓗ	Ⓙ
9.	Ⓐ	Ⓑ	Ⓒ	Ⓓ
10.	Ⓕ	Ⓖ	Ⓗ	Ⓙ
11.	Ⓐ	Ⓑ	Ⓒ	Ⓓ
12.	Ⓕ	Ⓖ	Ⓗ	Ⓙ
13.	Ⓐ	Ⓑ	Ⓒ	Ⓓ
14.	Ⓕ	Ⓖ	Ⓗ	Ⓙ
15.	Ⓐ	Ⓑ	Ⓒ	Ⓓ

Generalizing

Directions: Read the passage. Then read each question about the passage. Choose the best answer to each question. Mark the letter for the answer you have chosen.

Born to Fly

When Beryl Markham was just three, her parents left England to start a farm in Kenya, East Africa. Most European farmers were quite successful in Kenya, but Beryl's father found his talent in breeding and training horses.

Beryl's life was always full of interesting adventures. While some daughters of European farmers may have been sent to school in England, Beryl was raised in Africa. She learned to speak several African languages and hunted wild game with a spear. She became a horse trainer like her father. Later, she learned to fly an airplane and became a bush pilot.

Few women in the 1930s had the adventures that Beryl did. She became the first person to fly a plane solo nonstop from London to North America. She wrote a best-selling book about her experiences called *West with the Night*.

1. Which word in the first paragraph signals a generalization?
   A. when
   B. most
   C. Kenya
   D. just

2. Which of the following statements is a valid generalization from the first paragraph?
   F. Beryl's parents moved when she was three.
   G. Her father became a horse breeder and trainer.
   H. Her father always disliked farming.
   J. Most European farmers did quite well in Kenya.

3. Which word in the second paragraph signals a generalization?
   A. while
   B. always
   C. later
   D. full

4. Which of these statements is a faulty generalization?
   F. Beryl had many adventures.
   G. Beryl was raised in Africa.
   H. All horse trainers learn to fly.
   J. Flying was one of Beryl's many adventures.

5. Which word in the last paragraph signals a generalization?
   A. few
   B. fly
   C. wrote
   D. nonstop

Notes for Home: Your child read a passage and identified valid and faulty generalizations. *Home Activity:* Challenge your child to use words like *always, sometimes, never,* or *all* to make a generalization. Discuss whether this generalization is accurate (valid) or not (faulty).

Word Study: Plural Possessives

Directions: To make most words possessive, add an **apostrophe (')** and **s: the dog's bone.** For plural nouns that end in **-s**, just add the **apostrophe ('): the two dogs' bones.** Complete the table by writing the plural form and the plural possessive form of each noun.

Singular Noun	Plural Noun	Plural Possessive Noun
grandmother	1.	5.
house	2.	6.
teacher	3.	7.
Mr. Reed/Mrs. Reed	4. The	8. The

Directions: Read the paragraph below. You will see many words with apostrophes, including contractions and singular possessives. Find the words that are plural possessives. Circle each plural possessive and write it on the line.

Imagine traveling to the Arctic. You'll have to pack warm clothing to keep out the Arctic's cold. You'll travel on an icebreaker. The ship's prow is built like a snow plow, using heavy blades to break through the ice. Each day's adventures will fill you with wonder. You might hear polar bears' roars or seals' barks. The icebergs' incredible sizes are breathtaking. Watch out for ice floes! The floes' instability often causes crashes. Don't miss gazing at the night sky. The stars' brilliance is amazing, and the Northern Lights' colors dance. Imagine the early explorers' experiences as they first set foot upon this snowy wilderness.

9. _____

10. _____

11. _____

12. _____

13. _____

14. _____

15. _____

Notes for Home: Your child wrote and identified plural possessive nouns, such as: *the dogs' bone.* **Home Activity:** Read a story with your child. Point out words with apostrophes, and decide if they are possessives. Next, ask your child if they are plural possessives.

Atlas/Map

An **atlas** is a book of maps. A **map** is a drawing of a place. Maps have keys that show what the symbols on the maps mean. A compass shows directions north, south, east, and west. There are many kinds of maps. A picture map shows a place. A road map shows different types of roads. A political map shows city, state, and national boundaries. Physical maps show landforms, such as mountains and valleys. Special purpose maps may show specific information about a subject.

Directions: Admiral Peary made many attempts to reach the North Pole. This map shows the routes he took for each expedition, or trip, and the years he made each attempt. It lists the people who assisted him. Use the map to answer the questions on the next page.

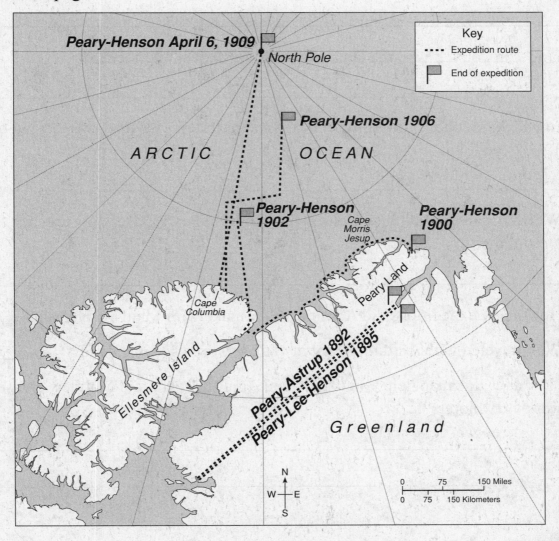

Name _____

1. What special purpose does this map have? _____

_____

2. What do the dashed lines on the map represent? _____

_____

3. What do the flag symbols on the map represent? _____

_____

4. Why is it important to study the map key? _____

_____

_____

5. How can you tell who made each expedition shown on the map?

_____

6. In which directions did Admiral Peary and Matthew Henson travel during their 1906 expedition to the North Pole?

_____

7. Which ocean did Matthew Henson and Admiral Peary travel over to reach the North Pole?

_____

8. How many expeditions did Admiral Peary make with Matthew Henson? _____

9. Who traveled with Admiral Peary in 1892 to northern Greenland? _____

10. How does this map help you understand Admiral Peary and Matthew Henson's work as explorers?

_____

_____

Notes for Home: Your child read a map and answered questions about it. *Home Activity:* Ask your child to draw a map showing the route he or she takes to school. Have your child include a key that explains any symbols, such as a symbol for a post office, bridge, or school.

Author's Purpose

- An **author's purpose** is the reason for writing something.
- Some purposes for writing are to entertain, to inform, to express, and to persuade.

Directions: Reread "Saving Our Wetlands." Then use the questions to help you determine the author's purpose or purposes for the article.

Questions	Answers
Title: What do the title and the subhead reveal about the author's purpose?	1.
Organization: How does the article's organization help you figure out the author's purpose?	2.
Key Words and Phrases: What key words or phrases does the author use that show how he feels about the wetlands?	Wetlands are home to many of the United States' birds.
	3.
	4.

Author's Purpose or Purposes

5. _____

_____

Notes for Home: Your child read a story and used story details to determine the author's purpose. *Home Activity:* With your child, read the editorial page of a newspaper. Ask him or her to find places where the writers inform, entertain, express, and persuade.

Vocabulary

Directions: Choose the word from the box that best matches each definition. Write the word on the line.

_____ 1. bottom side

_____ 2. broad, flat animal body part used for swimming

_____ 3. a flow of water

_____ 4. uncomfortable; uncoordinated

_____ 5. raised narrow strips

_____ 6. body tissues that move body parts

Directions: Choose the word from the box that best completes each sentence. Write the word on the matching numbered line to the right.

Molly dove beside the **7.** _____ reef into the warm ocean. The ocean's **8.** _____ was strong, but Molly was a good swimmer. Because she swam every day, she had strong **9.** _____ in her legs and arms. Sometimes she felt **10.** _____ and clumsy on land, but she never felt that way in the water.

7. _____

8. _____

9. _____

10. _____

Write a Description

On a separate sheet of paper, write a description of life under the ocean. You might want to find a picture in a book, encyclopedia, or magazine to help you visualize what ocean life is like. Use as many of the vocabulary words as you can in your description.

Notes for Home: Your child identified and used vocabulary words from *Into the Sea*. **Home Activity:** Talk with your child about the ocean, looking at pictures of it together if possible. Encourage your child to tell you how the vocabulary words are related to the ocean.

Author's Purpose

- An **author's purpose** is the reason or reasons an author has for writing.
- Four common purposes are to entertain, to inform, to express, and to persuade.

Directions: Reread *Into the Sea*. Then answer the question below.

1. What do you think was the author's purpose or purposes for writing this story? Give examples from the story to support your answer.

_____

_____

Directions: Read each paragraph. Write the author's purpose on the line after each paragraph and explain your answers.

2. Tony had a "Come as a Turtle" party. Tony's dad came as a sea turtle with a HUGE foam shell, woolly arms and legs, and a ski-mask head. He had to take off the shell to sit down!

_____

3. One of the really cool things about going canoeing is seeing painted turtles sunning themselves on logs. They look like kings. Their bodies seem to be covered in jewels that sparkle in the sun.

_____

4. Basking turtles live in ponds, streams, lakes, and marshes. They spend most of their time in the water, but they also bask in the sun. Their bodies are encased in bony shells.

_____

5. Choose your favorite story. On a separate sheet of paper, describe the author's purpose. Support your answer with examples from the story.

© Scott Foresman 4

Notes for Home: Your child read several passages and identified the author's purpose. ***Home Activity:*** With your child, look through books, magazines, and newspapers. Find an example of writing for each of the four common purposes listed above.

Name_____

1.	Ⓐ	Ⓑ	Ⓒ	Ⓓ
2.	Ⓕ	Ⓖ	Ⓗ	Ⓙ
3.	Ⓐ	Ⓑ	Ⓒ	Ⓓ
4.	Ⓕ	Ⓖ	Ⓗ	Ⓙ
5.	Ⓐ	Ⓑ	Ⓒ	Ⓓ
6.	Ⓕ	Ⓖ	Ⓗ	Ⓙ
7.	Ⓐ	Ⓑ	Ⓒ	Ⓓ
8.	Ⓕ	Ⓖ	Ⓗ	Ⓙ
9.	Ⓐ	Ⓑ	Ⓒ	Ⓓ
10.	Ⓕ	Ⓖ	Ⓗ	Ⓙ
11.	Ⓐ	Ⓑ	Ⓒ	Ⓓ
12.	Ⓕ	Ⓖ	Ⓗ	Ⓙ
13.	Ⓐ	Ⓑ	Ⓒ	Ⓓ
14.	Ⓕ	Ⓖ	Ⓗ	Ⓙ
15.	Ⓐ	Ⓑ	Ⓒ	Ⓓ

Selection Test

Directions: Choose the best answer to each item. Mark the letter for the answer you have chosen.

Part 1: Vocabulary

Find the answer choice that means about the same as the underlined work in each sentence.

1. The fish's mouth has <u>ridges</u>.
   - A. sharp teeth
   - B. spots of color
   - C. moving parts
   - D. raised, narrow strips

2. The fish swam with the <u>current</u>.
   - F. type of shark
   - G. group of seahorses
   - H. flow of water
   - J. large fishing nets

3. The young horse was <u>awkward</u>.
   - A. clumsy
   - B. watchful
   - C. tired
   - D. hungry

4. Baby birds need <u>protection</u>.
   - F. warm water
   - G. safety or defense
   - H. good food
   - J. friends or mates

5. We looked at the <u>coral</u> reef.
   - A. having valuable metals
   - B. from a sunken ship
   - C. filled with silver fish
   - D. made from skeletons of sea animals

6. Seals and whales have <u>flippers</u>.
   - F. keen senses
   - G. skin with thick layers of fat
   - H. eyes without lids
   - J. broad flat body parts used for swimming

7. We'll paint the boat's <u>underside</u>.
   - A. back section
   - B. bottom
   - C. wall
   - D. inside

8. The turtle's <u>muscles</u> are strong.
   - F. hard outer shells
   - G. gills used for breathing
   - H. habits or ways of behaving
   - J. tissues that move parts of the body

GO ON

Part 2: Comprehension

Use what you know about the selection to answer each item.

9. At the beginning of this selection, the turtle has just—
   A. hatched from an egg.
   B. eaten a crab.
   C. crawled out of the ocean.
   D. hidden from a fish.

10. For the first few months of its life, the turtle—
    F. builds a nest on a beach.
    G. drifts in a patch of seaweed.
    H. rests on the ocean floor.
    J. floats on the surface of water.

11. Which animal is still an enemy when the turtle is fully grown?
    A. sea gull
    B. butterfly fish
    C. shark
    D. remora

12. Getting caught in the net was dangerous for the turtle because—
    F. a whale had spotted her.
    G. she was almost out of breath.
    H. a man was pulling in the net.
    J. the net was cutting her shell.

13. The turtle returned to the island where it was born to—
    A. lay its eggs.
    B. escape from danger.
    C. find its favorite foods.
    D. prepare to die.

14. The author's main purpose in this selection is to—
    F. show how sea turtles and land turtles are different.
    G. tell a funny story about turtles.
    H. explain how people can help sea turtles.
    J. describe the life of a sea turtle.

15. The author probably thinks that sea turtles—
    A. must overcome many difficulties to survive.
    B. are the most intelligent animals in the world.
    C. take excellent care of their young.
    D. are gentle, friendly creatures.

STOP

Summarizing and Steps in a Process

Directions: Read the passage. Then read each question about the passage. Choose the best answer to each question. Mark the letter for the answer you have chosen.

Turtle Watching

Turtle watching may not be as exciting as whale watching, but you don't have to live near the ocean to do it.

Here's how to find a turtle. If you live where the winter is cold, you must first wait for spring. Then pick a sunny day. Choose a nearby stream with a soft bottom, a lake, a pond, a marsh, or a swamp. There should be a lot of plants. Turtles like them.

After you've chosen a good spot, take an adult with you. Travel on foot or in a small boat. Either way, be quiet. Don't make any sudden moves.

Finally, look for a rock or a log sticking out of the water. You just may see a turtle on it.

Now what? If you want to find out what kind of turtle you are looking at, well, that's another story.

1. The first thing you must do if you want to go turtle watching is—
   A. buy a telescope.
   B. get a boat.
   C. find a stream.
   D. be sure it is not too cold.

2. The next thing you should do is—
   F. learn all you can about turtles.
   G. pick a sunny day.
   H. travel in a boat.
   J. look for a rock.

3. To pick a spot, the first two things you should look for are—
   A. water and food.
   B. water and rocks.
   C. boats and people.
   D. water and plants.

4. Which of the following statements best summarizes the third paragraph?
   F. After finding a location, travel quietly and carefully with an adult by boat or on foot.
   G. Take an adult with you.
   H. Be quiet and don't move.
   J. Travel with an adult either on foot or by small boat.

5. Which clue word signals the last step in finding turtles?
   A. then
   B. after
   C. finally
   D. now

Notes for Home: Your child used story details to recognize steps in a process and to summarize the main idea of a passage. ***Home Activity:*** Together, tell a story about an activity you and your child do. Include steps to follow to do the activity.

Name _____

Phonics: Schwa Sound

Directions: The **schwa sound** is an indistinct vowel sound heard in an unstressed syllable. The **a** in **against** and the **o** in **fav<u>o</u>rite** are examples of the schwa sound. Read each word below. Underline the schwa sound in each word.

1. <u>a</u>lone
2. diff<u>i</u>cult
3. mom<u>e</u>nt
4. <u>a</u>round
5. season<u>a</u>l

6. del<u>i</u>cate
7. bott<u>o</u>m
8. <u>a</u>cross
9. sargass<u>u</u>m
10. s<u>u</u>rround

11. trop<u>i</u>cal
12. <u>o</u>ppose
13. cow<u>a</u>rd
14. <u>a</u>ccuse
15. c<u>o</u>mpete

Directions: Read each sentence below. Say the underlined word carefully to yourself. Listen for the schwa sound. Write the word on the line. Circle the letter or letters that represent the schwa sound.

_____ 16. The more I learn about sea animals, the more <u>amazed</u> I am at how clever they are.

_____ 17. For example, some sea animals float with the ocean's <u>currents</u> as they migrate.

_____ 18. Some small sea animals <u>attach</u> themselves to larger ones to catch a ride.

_____ 19. Some sea creatures survive by eating small bits of <u>plankton</u> that float in the water.

_____ 20. Many sea animals <u>camouflage</u> themselves, using their colors to blend in with their environment.

Notes for Home: Your child identified letters that represent the schwa sound, such as the *a* in *against* and the *o* in *fav<u>o</u>rite*. **Home Activity:** Read a story with your child. List words with two or more syllables that have the schwa sound. You can check these words in a dictionary.

© Scott Foresman 4

Diagram/Scale Drawing/ Pictures and Captions

A **diagram** is a special drawing with labels. Diagrams often show how something is made or how it works. A **scale drawing** is a diagram that uses a mathematical scale to help you determine the actual size of the subject. For example, a scale of 1 inch = 1 foot means that one inch on the drawing represents one foot in real life.

Directions: Use this diagram of the skeleton of a sea turtle to answer the questions that follow.

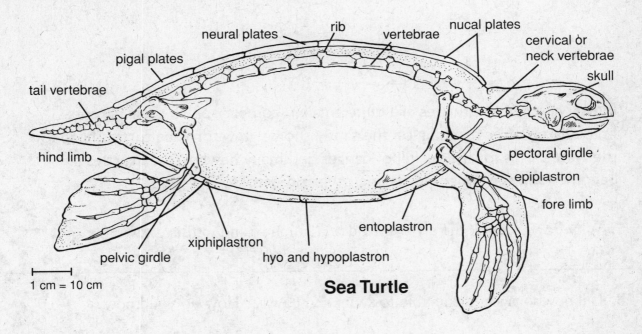

Sea Turtle

1. One centimeter on the drawing equals how many centimeters on a turtle? _____

2. About how long is the tail vertebrae of a real sea turtle? _____

3. Where are a sea turtle's nucal plates: near the neck, on the back, or near the tail?

_____

4. The vertebrae begin at the neck. Where do they end? _____

5. What is the name of the bone that forms the sea turtle's head? _____

6. A sea turtle has two girdles that help support its shell. What are the full names of the two girdles?

_____

Pictures are photographs or artwork that tell information about characters and events in a story or an article. They can also help set a mood. Sometimes pictures have captions that explain what is happening in a drawing or photograph.

Directions: Use the picture and the caption to answer the questions that follow.

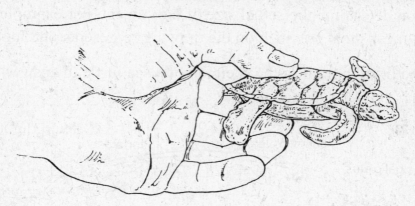

Newly hatched sea turtles are quite small in comparison to their parents. Immediately after hatching on the sandy shores, newborn sea turtles head for the water. This journey is full of danger and many newborn sea turtles become food for hungry birds and other predators.

7. Why do you think the artist included a human hand in this drawing?

_____

8. Is a newborn sea turtle able to swim right away? How do you know?

_____

9. Why is the trip from the hatching site to the sea a dangerous one for newborn sea turtles?

_____

_____

10. Why is it important to read the labels, scales, and captions for pictures carefully?

_____

_____

Notes for Home: Your child answered questions about a scale drawing and a picture with a caption. ***Home Activity:*** Ask your child to read captions from newspaper photos and tell you what information the captions provide.

Text Structure

- **Text structure** is the way a piece of writing is organized. The two main kinds of writing are fiction and nonfiction.
- Nonfiction tells about the real world. Some ways to organize nonfiction are cause and effect, problem and solution, and compare and contrast.

Directions: Reread the opening passage from *Space Probes to the Planets*. Then answer the questions below.

Have you ever wanted to visit another planet? Ever since the planets were discovered, people have dreamed of visiting them. But the planets are all very hot or very cold, and very far away. Until scientists learn more, a trip to explore them would be unsafe.

In the meantime we've learned a lot about the planets, partly because of space probes. Space probes are spacecraft with no people on them. With the help of computers and radio signals, they can travel to the planets by themselves.

SPACE PROBES TO THE PLANETS by Fay Robinson. Text copyright © 1993 by Fay Robinson.
Excerpt reprinted by permission of Albert Whitman & Company.

1. Why would a trip to the planets be unsafe?

   _____

2. How have scientists learned about the planets if they couldn't send people to explore them?

   _____

3. Why is it safe to use space probes?

   _____

4. Which kind of organization does this passage use: cause and effect, problem and solution, or compare and contrast? Explain.

   _____

   _____

5. Look at the rest of the story. Choose a passage and tell how it is organized. Write your answer on a separate sheet of paper.

Notes for Home: Your child used story details to identify the ways the text was organized. *Home Activity:* Go to the library with your child and find examples of fiction and nonfiction books about space exploration. Discuss how the writing is organized in each book.

Name_____

1.	Ⓐ	Ⓑ	Ⓒ	Ⓓ
2.	Ⓕ	Ⓖ	Ⓗ	Ⓙ
3.	Ⓐ	Ⓑ	Ⓒ	Ⓓ
4.	Ⓕ	Ⓖ	Ⓗ	Ⓙ
5.	Ⓐ	Ⓑ	Ⓒ	Ⓓ
6.	Ⓕ	Ⓖ	Ⓗ	Ⓙ
7.	Ⓐ	Ⓑ	Ⓒ	Ⓓ
8.	Ⓕ	Ⓖ	Ⓗ	Ⓙ
9.	Ⓐ	Ⓑ	Ⓒ	Ⓓ
10.	Ⓕ	Ⓖ	Ⓗ	Ⓙ
11.	Ⓐ	Ⓑ	Ⓒ	Ⓓ
12.	Ⓕ	Ⓖ	Ⓗ	Ⓙ
13.	Ⓐ	Ⓑ	Ⓒ	Ⓓ
14.	Ⓕ	Ⓖ	Ⓗ	Ⓙ
15.	Ⓐ	Ⓑ	Ⓒ	Ⓓ

Take Notes/Record Findings

Taking notes and **recording findings** of what you have read can help you when you are collecting information for a report. It can also help you keep track of information in a story and remember what you have read for a test.

There is no right or wrong way to take notes, but keep these points in mind:

- When you take notes, put what you read into your own words.
- If you're taking notes about a story, include the main characters' names and what you learn about them.
- Include only important details. Use key words, phrases, or short sentences.
- If you're taking notes for a report, be sure to include the source of your information.
- Read over your notes immediately after writing them to make sure you understand them.

Directions: Read the following article about women in space. Record notes on the following page as you read. Then use your notes to summarize the article.

Women have made great contributions to our exploration of space. Did you know that the first woman in space was Valentina Tereshkova? Her flight was on June 16, 1963. She flew in the Soviet spacecraft *Vostok 6*. She spent three days orbiting Earth. Svetlana Savitskaya became the second woman in space in 1982. She was also part of the Soviet space program.

On June 18, 1983, Sally Kristen Ride became the first American woman into space. Sally Ride worked on the *STS-7* and *STS-41-G* space missions. These missions conducted experiments and worked on communication satellite systems.

Since Sally Ride's voyages into space, there have been many women to follow. Shannon Lucid is the woman who has spent the most time in space—more than 222 days. Her first flight was June 1, 1985. Her last flight was March 22, 1996. On this mission, Shannon Lucid spent 188 days in space. This is the longest flight for any U.S. astronaut. She spent this time on the Russian space station *Mir* conducting science experiments.

Name _____

Notes

1. _____

_____

2. _____

_____

3. _____

_____

4. _____

_____

5. _____

_____

6. _____

_____

7. _____

_____

8. _____

_____

9. _____

_____

Summary

10. _____

_____

_____

Notes for Home: Your child recorded notes about an article and used these notes to summarize it. *Home Activity:* Have your child take notes while reading a newspaper article or watching a TV program. Have your child use the notes to summarize the article or show.

Visualizing

- **Visualizing** means forming a mental image as you read. To help visualize, look for details that tell how things look, smell, sound, taste, and feel.

Directions: Reread what happens in "Koya's Cousin Del." Then answer the questions below.

After dinner, the family gathered in the living room to listen to a tape of Delbert's next album. He had brought it to them as a gift.

"It won't be released until summer," he said. He got up and began dancing. "This is the latest thing from us folks up in the big city."

Koya glanced at her mother and was suprised to see that she was smiling. She never let them dance on the carpet. Whenever she caught them doing it, she would point toward the basement, and they knew they had better get down to the rec room, or they'd be sorry.

From KOYA DELANEY AND THE GOOD GIRL BLUES by Eloise Greenfield. Copyright © 1992 by Eloise Greenfield. Reprinted by permission of Scholastic Inc.

1. Picture the way the family looks as they gather in the living room. How do you think they look?

_____

2. Picture Delbert's face as he begins to dance. Describe how you think his face appears.

_____

_____

3. What sounds can you imagine as Delbert dances?

_____

_____

4. How do you imagine the carpet looks in the living room?

_____

5. Find another place in the story where you get a strong mental image of a scene. On a separate sheet of paper, write a paragraph describing what you visualize.

Notes for Home: Your child created a mental picture of the passage. *Home Activity:* Ask your child to picture a special place he or she has been. Invite your child to describe what he or she sees when imagining this place.

1.	Ⓐ	Ⓑ	Ⓒ	Ⓓ
2.	Ⓕ	Ⓖ	Ⓗ	Ⓙ
3.	Ⓐ	Ⓑ	Ⓒ	Ⓓ
4.	Ⓕ	Ⓖ	Ⓗ	Ⓙ
5.	Ⓐ	Ⓑ	Ⓒ	Ⓓ
6.	Ⓕ	Ⓖ	Ⓗ	Ⓙ
7.	Ⓐ	Ⓑ	Ⓒ	Ⓓ
8.	Ⓕ	Ⓖ	Ⓗ	Ⓙ
9.	Ⓐ	Ⓑ	Ⓒ	Ⓓ
10.	Ⓕ	Ⓖ	Ⓗ	Ⓙ
11.	Ⓐ	Ⓑ	Ⓒ	Ⓓ
12.	Ⓕ	Ⓖ	Ⓗ	Ⓙ
13.	Ⓐ	Ⓑ	Ⓒ	Ⓓ
14.	Ⓕ	Ⓖ	Ⓗ	Ⓙ
15.	Ⓐ	Ⓑ	Ⓒ	Ⓓ

Setting

Directions: Read the story. Then read each question about the story.
Choose the best answer to each question. Mark the letter for the answer you have chosen.

A Difficult Concert

Randall and his band got to the auditorium two hours later than planned. It was a cold day, and the roads were icy. Randall had to drive extra carefully to avoid an accident.

While they were driving, Randall had switched on the radio in the van. "Hello, out there!" said the disk jockey cheerfully. "We're going to start our countdown of the year's greatest hits!"

When the band finally got to the auditorium, the crowd was restless. They stamped so hard, the wooden bleachers shook. Even the basketball hoops were shaking. The band ran out onto the stage. "Greetings, everybody!" Randall shouted. "How are things here in Central Valley?"

The crowd cheered. "Are you ready for the year 2000?" he cried. "Here's a song to celebrate the last night of the old year!"

1. Based on the information in the story, what season is it?
   A. summer
   B. winter
   C. fall
   D. spring

2. How is Randall affected by the setting during the band's drive?
   F. He is shivering and uncomfortable.
   G. He puts on an extra sweater.
   H. He drives more slowly.
   J. He doesn't want to perform.

3. What else is the auditorium used for?
   A. a gym
   B. a cafeteria
   C. a town meeting hall
   D. school meetings

4. In what year does the story take place?
   F. 2001
   G. 1899
   H. 2000
   J. 1999

5. What holiday is coming up?
   A. Homecoming
   B. Presidents' Day
   C. Thanksgiving
   D. New Year's Day

Notes for Home: Your child identified a story's setting—the time and place where it occurs.
Home Activity: Ask your child to identify a favorite book, movie, or television show. Then ask him or her to tell you when and where the story takes place and tell you how he or she knows.

Name_____

Koya's Cousin Del

Word Study: Complex Spelling Patterns

Word List				
steady	reindeer	niece	caught	said
again	veil	brought	piece	bread

Directions: Some letter combinations, such as **ei, ie, ai, ea,** and **gh,** are hard to remember and spell correctly. Read the words in the box. Listen and look for similar letter combinations. Write each word in the correct column.

Words with ei

1. _____

2. _____

Words with ie

3. _____

4. _____

Words with ai

5. _____

6. _____

Words with ea

7. _____

8. _____

Words with gh

9. _____

10. _____

Directions: Choose the word from the box that best completes each sentence. Write the word on the line to the left. Not all the words will be used.

_____ 11. "The winter concert has started," _____ one parent.

_____ 12. "I can hear the _____ beat of the school's drummer," the other parent agreed.

_____ 13. Opening the door of the auditorium _____ the holiday music into the school corridor.

_____ 14. The children came out singing, dressed as silly _____.

_____ 15. "I think I can recognize my _____ under the horns and bright red nose," said the girl's uncle.

Notes for Home: Your child practiced words with complex spelling patterns. *Home Activity:* Encourage your child to keep a list of words he or she has trouble spelling correctly. Set aside time each week to practice spelling these words with your child.

© Scott Foresman 4

Poster/Advertisement

A **poster** is a kind of announcement that gives specific facts about an event. It usually answers the questions "Who?" "What?" "When?" "Where?" "Why?"

Directions: This poster gives information about a rock concert. Use the poster to answer the questions that follow.

Sunfruit Soft Drinks Present:

The Howling Wolf Pack

Friday, April 26th, 8:00 P.M.

The Whitamore Center, 125 Fairchild Ave.,
906 - 555 - 8364

Tickets cost $15 – $25

*Opening performance will be
by the Rainbow Rockers.*

1. What is the name of the main group performing? _____

2. What is the name of the group that will be performing first? _____

_____

3. Where is the concert? _____

4. What date is the concert? _____

5. Which ticket do you think costs $25—a ticket for a seat close to the stage or far away from the stage? Explain.

_____

_____

An **advertisement** is a kind of announcement that can be found in print or electronic media. The goal of an advertisement is to persuade readers, listeners, or viewers to do something, buy something, or feel a particular way about something.

Directions: Use the video game advertisement to answer the questions that follow.

6. What is the purpose of this advertisement? _____
_____

7. How do the pictures support this purpose? _____
_____

8. How do the words support this purpose? _____
_____

_____

9. What do you need to have to play this game? _____
_____

10. Name one fact and one opinion from the advertisement. _____
_____

Notes for Home: Your child answered questions about a poster and an advertisement. **Home Activity:** Choose an advertisement from the newspaper or a commercial on television. Ask your child to point out some facts and some opinions that the advertisement presents.

Steps in a Process

- Telling the **steps in a process** is telling the order of steps to complete an action.
- Clue words like *first, next,* and *last* or numbers written by the steps can show when each step is done.

First
↓
| Next |
↓
| Last |

Directions: Reread "From Drawing to Carousel Critter." Then complete the flowchart. Put the steps listed in the box in the order they must be done to turn a drawing into a carousel critter.

Steps

Enlarge drawing.
Paint animal.
Carve foam animal.
Trace drawing onto foam.
Sand it smooth.
Cover with varnish.
Glue together to make "sandwich."
Add eyes, a mouth, and other details.
Fit pole between cutouts.
Add three coats of fiberglass.
Cut out shapes.

Enlarge drawing.
↓
1.
↓
2.
↓
3.
↓
4.
↓
5.
↓
6.
↓
7.
↓
8.
↓
9.
↓
10.

Notes for Home: Your child read a story and identified steps in a process—the steps needed to complete an action. *Home Activity:* Together, perform a simple household task, such as putting away groceries or washing dishes. Ask your child to identify each step as it is performed.

Vocabulary

Directions: Choose the word from the box that best matches each
clue. Write the word on the line.

Check the Words You Know
__ figures
__ polish
__ pottery
__ screens
__ symbol

_____   1. You make this out of clay.

_____   2. This is something you do to make
things shiny.

_____   3. People often put these on doors and
windows.

_____   4. This is used to represent something else.

_____   5. These are small pieces of finished pottery.

Directions: Choose the word from the box that best completes each sentence.
Write the word on the line to the left.

_____   6. Tyrone is a skilled potter who makes and sells all
different kinds of _____.

_____   7. Tyrone picked up one of the many little clay _____
that he had made.

_____   8. He began to _____ the object to give it a bright
shine.

_____   9. He placed the object next to a plate painted with a
_____ representing the sun.

_____   10. Outside, several children peered through the wire
_____ to watch Tyrone at work.

Write an Art Review

On a separate sheet of paper, write about a piece of pottery or sculpture, either one
you have seen or one you saw in a picture. Tell what the figure looks like and what
you like about it. Use as many vocabulary words as you can.

Notes for Home: Your child identified and used vocabulary words from "Children of Clay."
Home Activity: Invite your child to tell you what each vocabulary word means. Together,
write a definition for each word. Take turns using these words in sentences.

© Scott Foresman 4

Selection Test

Directions: Choose the best answer to each item. Mark the letter for the answer you have chosen.

Part 1: Vocabulary

Find the answer choice that means about the same as the underlined word in each sentence.

1. We used the <u>screens</u>.
   A. rolls of paper
   B. large bottles or jugs
   C. carving tools
   D. wires woven with small openings

2. He showed us the <u>figures</u>.
   F. forms or shapes
   G. materials or supplies
   H. large painted pictures
   J. chips of broken clay

3. Now I will <u>polish</u> the dish.
   A. harden by baking
   B. make smooth and shiny
   C. decorate with designs
   D. show or display

4. These pictures are <u>symbols</u>.
   F. hopes or dreams
   G. ideas shared by many people
   H. strong feelings
   J. things that stand for something else

5. Show us the <u>pottery</u>.
   A. glass dishes and plates
   B. metal pieces of art
   C. pots and dishes made of clay
   D. objects carved from wood

Part 2: Comprehension

Use what you know about the selection to answer each item.

6. The family in this selection lives in a—
   F. Pueblo village.
   G. log cabin.
   H. large city.
   J. ranch house.

7. Which step happens first?
   A. taking sticks out of the clay
   B. soaking the clay in water
   C. letting the clay dry
   D. wrapping the clay in cloths

8. Sand is added to the clay to—
   F. make the clay thicker.
   G. keep the clay from cracking when it dries.
   H. get rid of stones and twigs.
   J. make the clay shiny.

GO ON

9. Who is Clay-Old-Woman?
   A. the children's grandmother
   B. a woman in the village
   C. a pottery teacher
   D. a spirit the people believe in

10. What step comes next after the clay is formed into pots and figures?
    F. They are left to dry.
    G. They are polished.
    H. They are washed.
    J. They are painted.

11. A good polishing stone must be—
    A. light.
    B. smooth.
    C. pointed.
    D. large.

12. When pottery is "fired," it is—
    F. covered with hot wax.
    G. dipped in boiling water.
    H. baked to make it hard.
    J. left out in the hot sun.

13. The author's main purpose in this selection is to—
    A. persuade people to make pottery.
    B. tell how to choose well-made pottery.
    C. explain how one family makes pottery.
    D. describe the village of Santa Clara.

14. What makes this pottery special to the people who buy it?
    F. It has been sanded.
    G. Some of it is plain.
    H. It is made completely by hand.
    J. Food can be cooked in it.

15. Which sentence best describes the family in this selection?
    A. They spoil the children.
    B. They like to play tricks on one another.
    C. They love to have fun.
    D. They work well together.

STOP

Main Idea and Supporting Details

Directions: Read the passage. Then read each question about the passage. Choose the best answer to each question. Mark the letter for the answer you have chosen.

The Pueblo People

The Pueblo are one of the oldest peoples in North America. The Pueblo are descended from an even older Southwestern culture called the Anasazi, which is Navajo for "ancient ones." Their villages developed in what is now the Southwestern area of the United States, including parts of Arizona, New Mexico, Colorado, and Utah.

Pueblo means "village" in Spanish. Pueblo homes are apartment-like buildings made of stone or adobe. An underground room, called a *kiva,* is used for special ceremonies.

Today, pueblo villages may still be made of adobe or stone. Like the old villages, rooms are often added onto a building to make more room as a village grows. An entire village might live in one building. Unlike the earlier buildings, these modern-day Pueblo buildings often have windows and doors.

1. The main idea of the whole passage is that the Pueblo—
   A. live in apartments.
   B. have a long history.
   C. live in the Southwest.
   D. have special ceremonies.

2. A key word to the main idea in the first paragraph is—
   F. oldest.　　　H. Arizona.
   G. developed.　J. Utah.

3. The second paragraph tells about the Pueblo's—
   A. homes.
   B. economy.
   C. religious beliefs.
   D. ancestors.

4. The last paragraph—
   F. describes the Anasazi.
   G. compares old and modern Pueblo villages.
   H. explains how to make adobe bricks.
   J. describes the Pueblo people.

5. Which of the following does **not** support the main idea of the passage?
   A. The Pueblo are one of the oldest peoples in North America.
   B. The Pueblo are descendents of the Anasazi.
   C. Modern Pueblo villages are similar to old villages.
   D. A kiva is a room used for special ceremonies.

Notes for Home: Your child identified the main idea and details of a passage. *Home Activity:* Read a brief newspaper article about a local person, place, or event. Ask your child to tell you the main idea. Take turns telling details from the story.

Word Study: Irregular Plurals

Directions: Most plurals are formed by adding **-s** or **-es.** Some words change their spelling to become plural. Some words have the same singular and plural form. Both of these types of words are called **irregular plurals.** Read each word below. Write the plural form of the word on the line.

1. child _____

2. deer _____

3. sheep _____

4. man _____

5. moose _____

6. person _____

7. foot _____

8. fish _____

9. woman _____

10. goose _____

Directions: Each sentence below has two plural nouns. Circle the plural nouns in each sentence. Then write just the irregular plurals on the lines.

One day last summer we went to a shop where

two women make musical instruments. On

Saturdays, visitors could make something to play

too. We built shoe-box guitars, then tapped our feet

to the music we made. We sang songs about fish

swimming upstream and one funny song about a

humpback whale. People listened and sang along,

and the children had a lot of fun.

11. _____

12. _____

13. _____

14. _____

15. _____

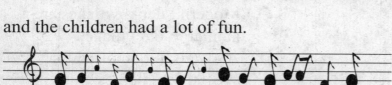

 Notes for Home: Your child wrote irregular plural words, such as *children, deer,* and *feet.* **Home Activity:** Write plural words on index cards. Include examples of irregular plurals. Ask your child to sort the words into two piles—regular and irregular.

© Scott Foresman 4

Dictionary

A **dictionary** is a book of words and their meanings. A **glossary** is a short dictionary at the back of some books that contain the definitions for words used in a specific book. You can use a **dictionary** or **glossary** to find a word's meaning.

Here are some things to know about using a dictionary:

- The words at the top of a dictionary page are called **guide words.** They show the first and last words on the page.
- If your word fits alphabetically between the two guide words, it is included on that page.
- When you find your word, you will see letters and symbols in parentheses. This **pronunciation key** tells how to say the word.
- The **definition** tells the meaning of the word. Choose the definition that makes the most sense in the sentence containing the word. Example sentences and illustrations may help define the word. Sometimes there is more than one meaning for a word.
- The **part of speech** tells how the word is used, such as a verb or noun.

Directions: Use these dictionary entries to answer the questions that follow.

---

polish/power

pol•ish (pol ´ ish), **1** to make or become smooth and shiny: *to polish shoes. The silverware polished beautifully.* **2** a substance used to give smoothness or shine: *silver polish.* **3** Smoothness or shininess: *The polish of the furniture reflected our faces like a mirror.* 1,2 *verb,* 2,3 *noun,* plural **po • lish • es.**

pot•ter•y (pot ´ ər ē), pots, dishes, or vases made from clay and hardened by heat. *noun.*

---

scrawl/script

scrawl (skrȯl), **1** to write or draw poorly or carelessly. **2** poor, careless handwriting. 1 *verb,* 2 *noun.*

scream (skrēm), **1** to make a loud, sharp, piercing cry. People scream in fright, in anger, and in excitement. **2** a loud, sharp, piercing cry. 1 *verb,* 2 *noun.*

---

1. What are the guide words for the page on which the entry word *scream* appears?

_____

2. What part of speech is listed for the third definition of *polish?* _____

3. How many syllables are in *pottery?* _____

4. What part of the entry for *polish* tells what the word sounds like? Write that part here.

_____

5. Does the *e* in *pottery* sound like the *e* in *scream?* _____

6. List one other word that might appear on a page that has *polish* and *power* as its guide words.

_____

7. What is the plural form of *polish?* _____

8. How many definitions does *scream* have? _____

9. What part of speech is listed for the first definition of *scream?* _____

10. How many definitions does *polish* have? _____

11. Which of the four words listed is used as a noun only? _____

12. List one word that might appear on the page just before the page with *scrawl.*

_____

13. How is the word *scrawl* used in the following sentence? *He scrawled his signature on the check.*

_____

14. Write the meaning of *scream* that is used in this sentence: *I scream every time I see a spider.*

_____

_____

15. Write a sentence using the third definition of *polish.*

_____

_____

Notes for Home: Your child practiced using a dictionary. ***Home Activity:*** Read a news article with your child and have him or her circle any unfamiliar words. Together, look up these words in a dictionary and discuss their meanings.

Fact and Opinion

- A **statement of fact** tells something that can be proved true or false.
- A **statement of opinion** tells your ideas or feelings. It cannot be proved true or false, but it can be supported by facts and reasons. Sometimes statements of opinion begin with clues such as *I believe.*

Directions: Reread the book review of *Naomi's Geese.* Then complete the tables. Identify statements of fact and statements of opinion from the review. Some have been done for you.

Fact
The book is about Naomi and two geese.
The reviewer's family moved to a lake in Maine.
1.
2.
3.

Opinion
I was worried about the loons.
I like how the geese called pieces of bread "fluffy white things."
4.
5.

Notes for Home: Your child read a book review and identified statements of fact and opinion. *Home Activity:* Choose a recent family event, such as a visit to a relative's house. Take turns telling statements of fact and opinion about the event.

Vocabulary

Directions: Choose the word from the box that best matches each
clue. Write the word on the line.

Check the Words You Know	
__ dreamer	
__ drifted	
__ heroes	
__ librarians	
__ rusty	
__ tremble	

_____   **1.** It's what your bike will become if
you leave it out in the rain.

_____   **2.** It's what you are if you spend more
time asleep than awake.

_____   **3.** These are people who do things
that other people admire.

_____   **4.** These are people who can't keep their hands off a
good book.

Directions: Choose the word from the box that best replaces each underlined word
or words. Write the word on the line.

_____   **5.** Traci had many <u>people she admired</u>.

_____   **6.** She loved books, and so she also admired <u>people
who ran libraries</u>.

_____   **7.** Traci was a <u>person who had a lot of dreams</u>.

_____   **8.** One day in the attic, she found an old metal box that
was <u>covered in rust</u>.

_____   **9.** She thought she had found a hidden treasure, and she
began to <u>shake</u> with excitement.

_____   **10.** The box held old postcards of an uncle who had
<u>wandered</u> from one interesting town to another.

Write a Poem

On a separate sheet of paper, write a poem about a wish or a dream. Use
vocabulary words in your poem.

Notes for Home: Your child identified and used vocabulary words from *Coming Home: From
the Life of Langston Hughes*. **Home Activity:** Ask your child to write six sentences, each one
including a different vocabulary word.

Fact and Opinion

- A **statement of fact** tells something that can be proved true or false.
- A **statement of opinion** tells your ideas or feelings. It cannot be proved true or false.

Directions: Reread what happens in *Coming Home: From the Life of Langston Hughes.* when Langston's mother comes to visit him. Then follow the instructions below.

Other times Langston's ma would come to Lawrence. Once it wasn't the best of times for her. Money was scarce. She snapped at Langston and it hurt.

Later that evening they went to St. Luke's Church where Langston's ma was giving a performance. She told him that she had a wonderful surprise for him. That he was going to be on the stage with her. That he was going to be a star, just like she was going to be.

Langston didn't like the surprise. That evening he was the one with the surprise. As his ma introduced him, behind her back Langston made faces: He crossed his eyes, stretched his mouth, and imitated her. Everyone burst out laughing.

From COMING HOME: FROM THE LIFE OF LANGSTON HUGHES by Floyd Cooper. Copyright © 1994 by Floyd Cooper. Reprinted by permission of Philomel Books, a division of Penguin Putnam Inc.

1. Tell whether this statement is fact or opinion: "Once it wasn't the best of times for her." Explain your answer.

   _____

2. Tell whether this statement is fact or opinion: "Money was scarce." Explain your answer.

   _____

3. Give a statement of fact from the second paragraph.

   _____

4. Tell an opinion that Langston's mother expresses in the second paragraph.

   _____

5. Reread the story. On a separate sheet of paper, write three statements of fact about Langston Hughes and two statements of opinion about him.

Notes for Home: Your child read a biography and identified statements of fact and opinion. *Home Activity:* Think of a recent family event, such as a party or visit from a relative. Ask your child to tell two facts and two opinions about the event.

1.	Ⓐ	Ⓑ	Ⓒ	Ⓓ
2.	Ⓕ	Ⓖ	Ⓗ	Ⓙ
3.	Ⓐ	Ⓑ	Ⓒ	Ⓓ
4.	Ⓕ	Ⓖ	Ⓗ	Ⓙ
5.	Ⓐ	Ⓑ	Ⓒ	Ⓓ
6.	Ⓕ	Ⓖ	Ⓗ	Ⓙ
7.	Ⓐ	Ⓑ	Ⓒ	Ⓓ
8.	Ⓕ	Ⓖ	Ⓗ	Ⓙ
9.	Ⓐ	Ⓑ	Ⓒ	Ⓓ
10.	Ⓕ	Ⓖ	Ⓗ	Ⓙ
11.	Ⓐ	Ⓑ	Ⓒ	Ⓓ
12.	Ⓕ	Ⓖ	Ⓗ	Ⓙ
13.	Ⓐ	Ⓑ	Ⓒ	Ⓓ
14.	Ⓕ	Ⓖ	Ⓗ	Ⓙ
15.	Ⓐ	Ⓑ	Ⓒ	Ⓓ

Selection Test

Directions: Choose the best answer to each item. Mark the letter for the answer you have chosen.

Part 1: Vocabulary

Find the answer choice that means about the same as the underlined word in each sentence.

1. The leaves began to <u>tremble</u>.
   A. move or shake
   B. grow quickly
   C. change color
   D. wither and die

2. The pot is <u>rusty</u>.
   F. large and heavy
   G. having many dents or bumps
   H. dripping or leaking
   J. covered with a reddish coating

3. Every child needs <u>heroes</u>.
   A. true friends
   B. admired persons
   C. wise teachers
   D. thoughtful adults

4. He has always been a <u>dreamer</u>.
   F. one who is usually sad
   G. person who acts young
   H. one who imagines how things might be
   J. person who causes harm

5. The <u>librarians</u> can help us.
   A. ideas that are written down
   B. persons who write books
   C. collections of things to read
   D. persons who work in libraries

6. People <u>drifted</u> through the park.
   F. moved easily or without care
   G. searched or looked about
   H. whispered or spoke softly
   J. rushed by

Part 2: Comprehension

Use what you know about the selection to answer each item.

7. Langston Hughes grew up in—
   A. Mexico.
   B. Kansas.
   C. Oklahoma.
   D. New York.

8. In his early years, Langston dreamed mostly of—
   F. becoming an actor.
   G. meeting famous people.
   H. learning to play jazz music.
   J. living with his pa and ma.

GO ON

9. You can tell from this selection that Langston's mother—
   A. cared a lot about her acting career.
   B. wanted Langston to be a dancer.
   C. liked living in different places.
   D. wanted Langston to be a writer.

10. How did Langston feel when he went to live with the Reeds?
   F. frightened and sad
   G. selfish and spoiled
   H. lonesome and bored
   J. happy and loved

11. Langston loved to tell his friends stories about—
   A. his mother and father.
   B. performing on stage.
   C. black people he admired.
   D. visiting the library.

12. Langston Hughes became a—
   F. writer.
   G. teacher.
   H. congressman.
   J. preacher.

13. Which sentence states a fact?
   A. "Living with Granma wasn't easy."
   B. "Auntie Reed's church was all right."
   C. "One day she took Langston all the way to Topeka to hear Booker T. Washington speak."
   D. "The singing and preaching felt so familiar."

14. Which sentence best describes Langston Hughes?
   F. He found home in his heart.
   G. He liked to be alone.
   H. He counted on other people to help him.
   J. He felt sorry for himself.

15. Which sentence states an opinion?
   A. Langston was chosen class poet.
   B. After school, he'd run and play with friends.
   C. Granma used to work on the Underground Railroad.
   D. Buffalo soldiers were the bravest of all.

STOP

Paraphrasing

Directions: Read the passage. Then read each question about the passage. Choose the best answer to each question. Mark the letter for the answer you have chosen.

Carl Sandburg: American Poet

Carl Sandburg wrote poems that found the beauty in ordinary people. His poetry shows his belief in "the common folk" and in their power to make the world a better place.

Sandburg worked many different jobs. For a while, he was a soldier. He did hard physical labor. He wrote for a newspaper. All of these experiences helped shape his poetry.

In addition to his poetry, Sandburg wrote a famous biography of President Abraham Lincoln. He also wrote children's books. The most famous is called *Rootabaga Stories*.

1. Sandburg wrote—
    A. long poems.
    B. poems about nature.
    C. poems about ordinary people.
    D. poems about famous people.

2. Sandburg's work—
    F. helped him write his poetry.
    G. prevented him writing poetry.
    H. was separate from his poetry.
    J. paid a lot of money.

3. Complete this paraphrase of the last paragraph: Sandburg also wrote —
    A. children's stories.
    B. a biography of Lincoln and children's stories.
    C. a biography of Lincoln.
    D. *Rootabaga Stories*.

4. Which detail would probably not be part of a paraphrase of the passage?
    F. Sandburg wrote poems about ordinary people.
    G. He worked many different jobs.
    H. He wrote children's books and a biography.
    J. He wrote *Rootabaga Stories*.

5. Complete this paraphrase of the whole passage: Carl Sandburg was an American poet who—
    A. worked at different jobs and wrote books as well as poetry.
    B. showed his belief in ordinary people through his writing.
    C. wrote a famous biography.
    D. worked many hard jobs.

Notes for Home: Your child read a passage and identified statements that paraphrased the passage's main ideas. ***Home Activity:*** Tell your child about something you did together today. Ask your child to paraphrase your story by retelling it in his or her own words.

Phonics: Consonant Sounds
/k/ and /f/

Word List				
books	enough	America	trophy	kitchen
family	beautiful	Kansas	tracks	Buffalo

Directions: Read the words in the box. Listen for words that have the sound /k/ and words that have the sound /f/. Write each word in the correct column.

Words with the sound /k/

1. _____

2. _____

3. _____

4. _____

5. _____

Words with the sound /f/

6. _____

7. _____

8. _____

9. _____

10. _____

Directions: Read each sentence below. Listen for the word that has the sound /k/ or /f/. Circle the word and write it on the line. Underline the letters that stand for the sound /k/ or /f/.

_____ **11.** As he played in his backyard, the young boy heard the whistle of the passing train.

_____ **12.** He ran to the fence to watch the train go by.

_____ **13.** "Someday, I hope to ride on the train," he said to himself.

_____ **14.** He listened to the clickety-clack of the wheels.

_____ **15.** He laughed and waved at people in the train.

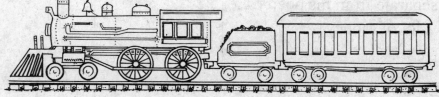

Notes for Home: Your child identified different letters that represent the sound /k/, *(c, k, ck)* and the sound /f/, *(f, ff, gh, ph)*. **Home Activity:** While reading with your child, take turns trying to find words with these two sounds.

Organize and Present Information/Draw Conclusions

Before you prepare a report, you need to organize your information. For example, you might make a story map to record ideas about plot, setting, and characters in a story. You might use a cluster web to show facts and details about a person, place, or thing.

Directions: Reread *Coming Home*. Then complete the cluster web to give facts and details that you learned about Langston Hughes. Then answer the question that follows.

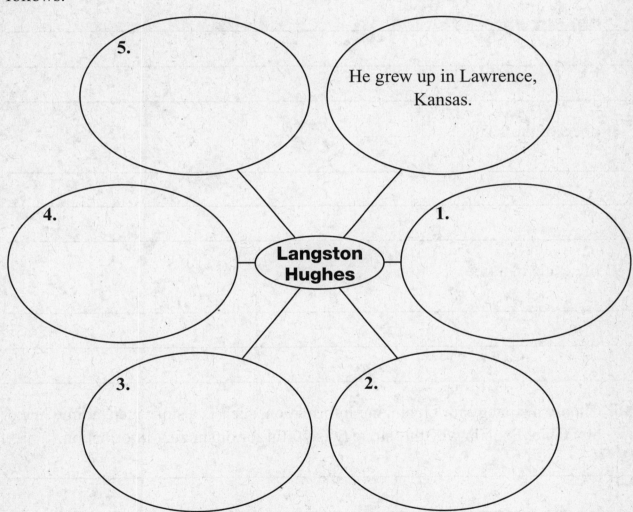

5.

He grew up in Lawrence, Kansas.

4.

Langston Hughes

1.

3.

2.

6. Did you find it helpful to organize information in a cluster web? Explain.

_____

_____

_____

After you have collected information for a report, you have to present it to others. You could present your report orally, write a report or a story, draw a time line or make a drawing with captions. In your presentation, you should draw conclusions about the information you've organized to explain what it means.

Directions: Read each topic. Decide whether a written report, a time line, or a picture with captions would be the best method of presentation. Give an explanation to support each answer.

7. NASA space launches

_____

_____

_____

8. poets of the 1950s

_____

_____

_____

9. life cycle of a tree

_____

_____

_____

10. Choose a strategy for organizing information, such as a story map, a time line, or a table. Explain why this strategy is useful for organizing information.

_____

_____

_____

Notes for Home: Your child learned how to organize and present information. *Home Activity:* Work with your child to organize a story about his or her life. Use a time line to show important events. Have your child tell his or her story to family members or friends.

© Scott Foresman 4

Main Idea and Supporting Details

- The **topic** is what a paragraph or article is all about.
- The **main idea** is the most important idea about the topic. Sometimes it is stated, and sometimes you have to figure it out and put it into your own words.
- **Supporting details** are small pieces of information that tell more about the main idea.

Directions: Reread "Working on the Railroad." Then complete the diagram by finishing the sentences that tell about the article's main idea and some of its supporting details.

Main Idea
1. Because railroad work was difficult and dangerous,

↓

Supporting Details
2. The brakeman was in danger because
3. Andrew Beard created
4. Railroad firemen had to
5. Elijah McCoy invented

Notes for Home: Your child read an article and identified its main idea and some of its supporting details. *Home Activity:* Read a news article with your child. Together, identify the main idea of the article and take turns naming the supporting details.

Vocabulary

Directions: Choose the word from the box that best matches each definition. Write the word on the line.

_____ 1. chart showing months, weeks, days, and dates of a year

_____ 2. form of energy that can produce light, heat, or motion

_____ 3. hard to explain or understand

_____ 4. explanation based on observation and reasoning

_____ 5. a trial or a test to find out something

Check the Words You Know

__ almanac
__ calendar
__ circulating
__ electricity
__ experiment
__ inventions
__ mysterious
__ theory

Directions: Choose the word from the box that best matches each clue. Write the word on the line.

_____ 6. It has useful information.

_____ 7. This is what library books are doing.

_____ 8. These often become everyday tools, like toasters, automobiles, and computers.

_____ 9. This runs your refrigerator and lights your house.

_____ 10. Scientists use observation to help create this idea.

Write a Description

Imagine a new invention that would do some chore that you hate. On a separate sheet of paper, write a description of this invention and how it works. Use as many vocabulary words as you can.

Notes for Home: Your child identified and used vocabulary words from "Out of the Blue." *Home Activity:* Read each vocabulary word to your child and ask him or her to tell you what it means.

Main Idea and Supporting Details

- The **main idea** is the most important idea about the topic.
- **Supporting details** are small pieces of information that tell more about the main idea.

Directions: Reread the following passage in "Out of the Blue." Then answer the questions below.

Philadelphia suited young Benjamin perfectly. He lived on High Street, the busiest and noisiest street in town. On one end of the street was the Delaware River to jump into when he felt like a goat leap. On the other end of the street was Debbie Read, whom he courted and married.

Benjamin and Debbie were married in 1730. Benjamin was twenty-four years old now and getting ahead in the world. He had his own printshop, owned his own newspaper, and because he was such a good printer, he did the printing for the government of Pennsylvania. (He always used the blackest ink and the whitest paper he could find.) In addition, Debbie and Benjamin ran a store in the front of their house.

From WHAT'S THE BIG IDEA, BEN FRANKLIN? by Jean Fritz. Copyright © 1976 by Jean Fritz. Used by permission of Coward-McCann, Inc., a division of Penguin Putnam Inc.

1. What is the main idea in the first paragraph?

_____

2. Is the main idea in the first paragraph stated? Explain.

_____

3. What is the main idea in the second paragraph?

_____

4. What are two examples of supporting details in the second paragraph?

_____

_____

5. On a separate sheet of paper, tell the main idea of "Out of the Blue," and give two supporting details.

Notes for Home: Your child read a biography and identified its main ideas and supporting details. **Home Activity:** Read a newspaper article with your child. Ask your child to tell you the most important idea of the story. Take turns identifying supporting details.

1.	Ⓐ	Ⓑ	Ⓒ	Ⓓ
2.	Ⓕ	Ⓖ	Ⓗ	Ⓙ
3.	Ⓐ	Ⓑ	Ⓒ	Ⓓ
4.	Ⓕ	Ⓖ	Ⓗ	Ⓙ
5.	Ⓐ	Ⓑ	Ⓒ	Ⓓ
6.	Ⓕ	Ⓖ	Ⓗ	Ⓙ
7.	Ⓐ	Ⓑ	Ⓒ	Ⓓ
8.	Ⓕ	Ⓖ	Ⓗ	Ⓙ
9.	Ⓐ	Ⓑ	Ⓒ	Ⓓ
10.	Ⓕ	Ⓖ	Ⓗ	Ⓙ
11.	Ⓐ	Ⓑ	Ⓒ	Ⓓ
12.	Ⓕ	Ⓖ	Ⓗ	Ⓙ
13.	Ⓐ	Ⓑ	Ⓒ	Ⓓ
14.	Ⓕ	Ⓖ	Ⓗ	Ⓙ
15.	Ⓐ	Ⓑ	Ⓒ	Ⓓ

Selection Test

Directions: Choose the best answer to each item. Mark the letter for the answer you have chosen.

Part 1: Vocabulary

Find the answer choice that means about the same as the underlined word in each sentence.

1. Where is the new <u>calendar</u>?
   A. large, heavy book
   B. chart of months and days
   C. list of places to see
   D. book of telephone numbers

2. There was no <u>electricity</u>.
   F. form of energy
   G. equipment used by scientists
   H. disagreement
   J. chance for people to vote

3. The <u>inventions</u> worked.
   A. wise sayings
   B. things created or thought up
   C. money set aside and saved
   D. builders or carpenters

4. We will do an <u>experiment</u>.
   F. trial or test
   G. report
   H. performance
   J. job or chore

5. The <u>almanac</u> is amusing.
   A. daily journal kept to record a person's ideas and activities
   B. postcard or letter
   C. yearly publication of brief information on many subjects
   D. story book with pictures

6. She is a <u>mysterious</u> woman.
   F. very pretty
   G. old and wise
   H. highly skilled
   J. hard to understand

7. His <u>theory</u> interests me.
   A. training or education
   B. something made to be displayed
   C. way of behaving
   D. explanation based on observing

8. This is a <u>circulating</u> library book.
   F. popular or well liked
   G. passing from person to person
   H. easily torn or ripped
   J. uncommon or difficult to find

GO ON ➡

Part 2: Comprehension

Use what you know about the selection to answer each item.

9. In Philadelphia, Ben Franklin got a job with a—
   A. clothing maker.
   B. printer.
   C. watchmaker.
   D. sailor.

10. Members of the Leather Apron Club met every week to—
   F. talk about ideas.
   G. print newspapers.
   H. do experiments.
   J. make clothes.

11. You know that young Ben Franklin had many interests because he—
   A. went to work when he was 17.
   B. lived in Philadelphia.
   C. owned a printshop, a newspaper, and a store.
   D. made friends easily.

12. Publishing his almanac gave Ben Franklin a chance to—
   F. use his sense of humor.
   G. write about electricity.
   H. sell his inventions.
   J. tell how hurricanes move.

13. What is the main idea of this selection?
   A. Ben Franklin should have been a scientist.
   B. Ben Franklin improved the lives of people in Philadelphia.
   C. Most people liked Ben Franklin's ideas.
   D. Ben Franklin had many ideas, but his big one was that lightning is electricity.

14. Which sentence states an opinion?
   F. Electricity and lightning are the same.
   G. Lightning is as mysterious as heaven.
   H. Electricity is attracted to pointed iron rods.
   J. Ben Franklin felt an electric shock through a key tied to a kite.

15. In his lifetime, Ben Franklin was best known for his—
   A. magic squares.
   B. ideas about electricity.
   C. household inventions.
   D. writings about comets.

STOP

Generalizing

Directions: Read the story. Then read each question about the story. Choose the best answer to each question. Mark the letter for the answer you have chosen.

Lydia LaRue: Great Inventor

Lydia LaRue wanted to be a great inventor. Her first invention was a new kind of alarm clock. A rooster crowed, which was supposed to wake up a mouse, who started running on a little wheel. The little wheel made a ball fall into a glass of water. Being splashed by the water woke the person up.

The first day Lydia tried out her invention, the rooster overslept. The second day, the mouse didn't wake up. By the third day, the water had dried up.

Lydia's second invention was a special kind of washing machine. In the bottom of the machine were three big fish. They were supposed to swim and splash, moving the water. However, the fish got sick from the laundry soap, so Lydia set them free.

"I'll never give up," Lydia vowed. "A person who works hard can always succeed."

1. Which generalization about Lydia's inventions is valid?
   A. They are complicated.
   B. They are simple.
   C. They work well.
   D. They are expensive.

2. Which generalization about Lydia's inventions is faulty?
   F. They involve electricity.
   G. They involve animals.
   H. They involve water.
   J. They imitate existing machines.

3. Which generalization about Lydia's first invention is valid?
   A. Each part involved animals.
   B. Each part involved water.
   C. Each part involved electricity.
   D. Each part failed to work.

4. Which of the following statements is a generalization?
   F. Lydia has animals.
   G. Lydia invents machines.
   H. Lydia and Ben Franklin are both inventors.
   J. Complicated ideas often do not work.

5. What clue word tells you that Lydia's last statement is a generalization?
   A. I'll
   B. works
   C. hard
   D. always

Notes for Home: Your child identified valid, or accurate, generalizations and faulty, or inaccurate, generalizations. *Home Activity:* Use the words *always, never, sometimes,* and *most* to make a broad statement about several things that is a valid generalization.

Word Study: Suffixes

Directions: Letters added to the end of base words are called **suffixes.** Suffixes can change the meaning of the base words. Add a suffix to each word below to make a new word. Write each new word on the line. Hint: You might need to change some letters in the base word.

1. bright   +   -en   = _____

2. creative   +   -ity   = _____

3. educate   +   -ion   = _____

4. bother   +   -some   = _____

5. pass   +   -ive   = _____

6. transport   +   -ation   = _____

7. divide   +   -sion   = _____

Directions: Read each sentence below. Look for words that use one of the suffixes listed above. Write the word on the line. Then circle the suffix.

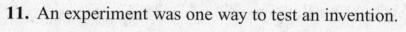
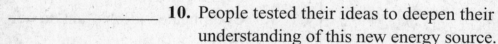

_____   **8.** Electricity was an amazing discovery.

_____   **9.** The need for a better source of energy was a strong motivation.

_____   **10.** People tested their ideas to deepen their understanding of this new energy source.

_____   **11.** An experiment was one way to test an invention.

_____   **12.** To be effective, an experiment must be carefully controlled.

_____   **13.** Much information can be gained by testing.

_____   **14.** The creation of the first light bulb is a day to remember.

_____   **15.** An inventor's hard work should never be viewed as troublesome.

Notes for Home: Your child built new words by adding suffixes such as *-en (lengthen).* **Home Activity:** Challenge your child to find words in print with suffixes. Start a three-column chart to write the base word, the suffix, and the word with the suffix added.

© Scott Foresman 4

Study Strategies

Study Strategies help you focus on the most important parts of what you read. **Skimming and scanning** are two ways of looking at written materials quickly, focusing only on important parts.

Skimming is looking at a story or article quickly to find out what it is about. When skimming, you do not read the entire story. You look for highlights, such as titles and captions. Skimming helps you decide whether you want to read the text and whether it is useful for your research and study purposes.

Scanning is looking for key words or ideas. You can scan when you need to answer a specific question. Read the sentences around the key words to find the answer to your question.

Directions: Skim the article on the next page to answer the questions below.

1. Who is the article about? _____

2. What can you learn by reading this article? _____

_____

_____

3. How many different inventions are mentioned? What are they? _____

_____

_____

4. Would you read this article if you needed information about things Thomas Jefferson did when he was the President of the United States? Explain.

_____

_____

5. Would you read this article if you needed information about important accomplishments Thomas Jefferson made in his lifetime? Explain.

_____

_____

Thomas Jefferson: Inventor

While Thomas Jefferson is mostly known for being a brilliant politician, he was also quite an inventor. Many of his inventions were items he used in his house. They were things that made life easier for him.

Revolving Closet

One of his inventions helped him get dressed in the morning. At the end of his bed he had a revolving closet. It was a long pole that reached from floor to ceiling. This pole had forty-eight arms. Each arm held one item of clothing. Jefferson could turn the arms with a long stick making it easier to find the clothes he wanted to wear.

Revolving Bookstand

Another item Jefferson is believed to have invented is a revolving bookstand. Jefferson joined five bookstands and placed them on a revolving platform. Using this device, he was able to review different books with ease.

The Great Clock

One of Jefferson's most impressive creations was his Great Clock. This clock had two faces. The outside face had only an hour hand. This, he felt, was all the information workers needed. Its gong chimed the hour loud enough to be heard from 3 miles away. The inside face had hour, minute, and second hands. The weights that moved the clock's hands also indicated the day of the week.

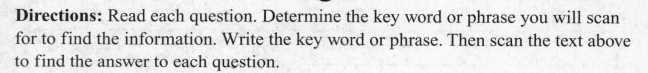

Directions: Read each question. Determine the key word or phrase you will scan for to find the information. Write the key word or phrase. Then scan the text above to find the answer to each question.

6. Which invention did Thomas Jefferson use to find clothes more easily?

_____

7. From how many miles away could the Great Clock chime be heard?

_____

8. Which invention did Thomas Jefferson use for reviewing several books at a time?

_____

9. What portion of the Great Clock did Jefferson feel was most useful for workers?

_____

10. What did the Great Clock's inside face show? _____

_____

Notes for Home: Your child skimmed and scanned an article to find necessary information quickly. **Home Activity:** Give your child a newspaper article you have read. Ask questions that can be answered by scanning (looking for key words) the article.

Name _____

Author's Purpose

- An **author's purpose** is the reason for writing something.
- Some purposes for writing are to entertain, to inform, to express, and to persuade.

Directions: Reread "Breakfast with Brede." Then complete the web. Identify the author's purpose and give four clues that helped you decide.

2. Grandpa says scones are like

3. Brede says scones are like camels'

4. Brede says scones are like elephants'

Author's Purpose or Purposes

1.

5. Why isn't Andrew allowed to finish speaking?

Notes for Home: Your child identified the author's purpose in a story. *Home Activity:* Ask your child to pick a favorite story. Ask him or her to identify the author's purpose. Then have your child support his or her answer with examples from the story.

Vocabulary

Directions: Choose the word from the box that best matches each definition. Write the word on the line.

_____ **1.** boast

_____ **2.** large printed sheet or notice on a wall

_____ **3.** point of view

_____ **4.** ability to project a sense of ease

_____ **5.** come near

Directions: Choose the word from the box that best completes each sentence. Write the word on the line to the left.

_____ **6.** Dottie is a detective who always has an interesting _____ on any problem.

_____ **7.** One day, Myron had lost a candy bar made from his favorite kind of _____.

_____ **8.** Right away, Dottie began to _____ to others that she could easily solve the mystery.

_____ **9.** Dottie's certainty and strong _____ made Myron believe that his candy bar would be found fast.

_____ **10.** "If you have seen the candy bar, come forward and _____ me," said Dottie. "There is a reward—another candy bar!"

Write a Detective Story

On a separate sheet of paper, tell the story of a classroom detective. Tell what the mystery is, who the detective is, and what he or she does to solve the mystery. Use as many vocabulary words as you can.

Notes for Home: Your child identified and used vocabulary words from "Chocolate Is Missing." *Home Activity:* With your child, act out the roles of a detective questioning a suspect. Try to use as many vocabulary words as you can.

© Scott Foresman 4

Name_____

Author's Purpose

> • An **author's purpose** is the reason or reasons the author has for writing.
> • Four common author's purposes are to entertain, to inform, to express, and to persuade.

1. Reread "Chocolate Is Missing." Tell what you think the author's purpose or purposes were for writing this story. Explain your answer.

_____

Directions: Tell what the author's purpose or purposes were for writing each passage below. Explain your answer.

2. I love my cat, Tomiddy. He snuggles up next to me when I read and keeps me company. When I'm feeling blue, I pick Tomiddy up and give him a big hug. I push my face into his soft, comforting fur. He purrs and purrs. A Tomiddy hug is good for cheering me up.

_____

3. Guinea pigs belong to a family of rodents that are native to South America. Other members of this family are rock cavies and mountain cavies. Rodents have unusually long, sharp front teeth that keep growing. Rodents' unusual ability to gnaw keeps their teeth sharp!

_____

4. *All Creatures Great and Small* is a wonderful book about an English veterinarian and his animal cases. The stories are interesting, and the book is well written and easy to read. If you like reading about animals, you really should look at this fascinating book.

_____

5. Think about other stories you have read in class. On a separate sheet of paper, name a story or article that was written for each of the four common purposes listed above. Explain your choices.

Notes for Home: Your child read several passages and identified the reason or reasons an author has for writing. *Home Activity:* Ask your child to think of a favorite book. Encourage him or her to tell you why the author wrote the book.

1.	Ⓐ	Ⓑ	Ⓒ	Ⓓ
2.	Ⓕ	Ⓖ	Ⓗ	Ⓙ
3.	Ⓐ	Ⓑ	Ⓒ	Ⓓ
4.	Ⓕ	Ⓖ	Ⓗ	Ⓙ
5.	Ⓐ	Ⓑ	Ⓒ	Ⓓ
6.	Ⓕ	Ⓖ	Ⓗ	Ⓙ
7.	Ⓐ	Ⓑ	Ⓒ	Ⓓ
8.	Ⓕ	Ⓖ	Ⓗ	Ⓙ
9.	Ⓐ	Ⓑ	Ⓒ	Ⓓ
10.	Ⓕ	Ⓖ	Ⓗ	Ⓙ
11.	Ⓐ	Ⓑ	Ⓒ	Ⓓ
12.	Ⓕ	Ⓖ	Ⓗ	Ⓙ
13.	Ⓐ	Ⓑ	Ⓒ	Ⓓ
14.	Ⓕ	Ⓖ	Ⓗ	Ⓙ
15.	Ⓐ	Ⓑ	Ⓒ	Ⓓ

Name _____

Selection Test

Directions: Choose the best answer to each item. Mark the letter for the answer you have chosen

Part 1: Vocabulary

Find the answer choice that means about the same as the underlined work in each sentence.

1. Jay has a different <u>angle</u>.
   A. point of view
   B. troubled or worried feeling
   C. person who offers help
   D. notebook divider

2. The girls looked at the <u>poster</u>.
   F. open drawer
   G. small card sent by mail
   H. secret message
   J. printed notice hung on a wall

3. Mr. Jones changed his <u>approach</u>.
   A. way of working on a task
   B. tone of voice
   C. time and place for a meeting
   D. way a person looks

4. I tried not to <u>brag</u>.
   F. complain
   G. become confused
   H. boast
   J. worry

5. Here is some <u>chocolate</u>.
   A. dark-gray color
   B. strong, sweet odor
   C. small box or container
   D. substance used in candies and other foods

6. Rena has great <u>presence</u>.
   F. duties or jobs
   G. ability to imagine
   H. gift given to another person
   J. sense of being sure of oneself

Part 2: Comprehension

Use what you know about the story to answer each item.

7. How is Gayle different from Lila?
   A. Gayle is taller and wider.
   B. Gayle cares more about Chocolate.
   C. Gayle is a better writer.
   D. Gayle is not as logical.

8. In this story, Chocolate is a—
   F. cat.
   G. guinea pig.
   H. snake.
   J. rabbit.

GO ON

9. What happened next after the class
   found that Chocolate was gone?
   A. Lila and Eddie looked for
      Chocolate.
   B. Lila and Gayle made posters.
   C. Lila realized Chocolate had
      escaped.
   D. Lila and Gayle talked to
      Michael.

10. The author probably included Lila's
    list of suspects to show—
    F. how smart Lila is.
    G. that Chocolate was stolen.
    H. that Lila was a bit silly.
    J. which students could not be
       trusted.

11. Lila was not ready to do her oral
    report because she—
    A. knew Mr. Sherman would
       understand how busy she was.
    B. did not want to talk in front of
       the class.
    C. forgot about it while searching
       for Chocolate.
    D. did not want to learn about
       Brazil.

12. Chocolate probably hid in Mr.
    Sherman's desk because she—
    F. found lots of food there.
    G. was afraid of the children.
    H. needed a safe place for her
       babies.
    J. was sick.

13. The author's main purpose in this
    selection is to—
    A. tell an amusing story.
    B. explain how to solve mysteries.
    C. describe a class of students.
    D. give tips for keeping class pets.

14. Near the end of the story, it is
    suggested that Lila was jealous of—
    F. Mr. Todd.
    G. Rita Morgan.
    H. Michael Watson.
    J. Eddie English.

15. Mr. Sherman was probably most
    impressed that Lila—
    A. pretended to be a detective.
    B. worked so hard to find
       Chocolate.
    C. knew so much about Brazil.
    D. was Gayle's best friend.

STOP

Plot

Directions: Read the story. Then read each question about the story. Choose the best answer to each question. Mark the letter for the answer you have chosen.

Penny's Parrot

All her life, Penny had lived in sunny southern California. When she heard that her family was moving to Alaska, Penny felt sad.

However, Penny soon discovered that she liked sledding and skating. She also liked her new friends at school.

But Penny's parrot seemed very sad. It was home alone all day in Penny's house. Penny discovered that parrots like warm weather! Penny's house was too cold during the day when no one was home.

Penny decided to bring her parrot to school. The parrot was happy with the warm classroom—and Penny's class had a new pet!

1. What happens to Penny at the beginning of the story?
   A. She moves to Alaska.
   B. She moves to California.
   C. She learns to skate.
   D. She gets a parrot.

2. What problem does Penny have?
   F. She hates the cold.
   G. She has no friends.
   H. Her parrot is sad.
   J. Her parrot is noisy.

3. What causes Penny's problem?
   A. Alaska is not a good place to live.
   B. The parrot doesn't like the cold house.
   C. Alaska is a big state.
   D. Penny is very shy.

4. How does Penny solve her problem?
   F. She feeds her parrot.
   G. She gives her parrot away.
   H. She makes new friends.
   J. She brings her parrot to school.

5. Why does this action solve Penny's problem?
   A. The class likes her better now.
   B. She doesn't have to take care of her parrot anymore.
   C. The parrot has a warmer place to live.
   D. Her parrot makes less noise.

Notes for Home: Your child answered questions about a story's plot. **Home Activity:** Plan a story with your child. Describe when and where the story will take place, who the characters are, what problem they'll face, and how they'll solve it.

Word Study: Word Building

Directions: Add a suffix to each word below to make a new word. Write each new word on the line. Hint: The spelling of some words may change slightly when the suffix is added. Use a dictionary if necessary.

1. explain + -ation = _____

2. imagine + -ation = _____

3. describe + -tion = _____

4. inform + -ation = _____

5. drama + -tic + -al + -ly = _____

Directions: Read each word below. Write each base word and suffix in the correct column. Remember to adjust the spelling of the base word if needed.

Word		Base Word		Suffix
6. interrogation	=	_____	+	_____
7. nomination	=	_____	+	_____
8. investigation	=	_____	+	_____
9. maintenance	=	_____	+	_____
10. rectangular	=	_____	+	_____

Directions: Sometimes when a suffix is added to a base word, some sounds in the word change. Read the pairs of words below. Listen for the syllable that is stressed. Underline the stressed syllable in each word, for example: **mu<u>sic</u>** and **mu<u>si</u>cian.**

11. nominate   nomination

12. maintain   maintenance

13. interrogate   interrogation

14. rectangle   rectangular

15. investigate   investigation

Notes for Home: Your child listened for the ways in which words can change when a suffix is added. **Home Activity:** With your child, think of words that have suffixes. Clap each syllable as you say the word, clapping more loudly for the one that is stressed.

Technology: Electronic Media

There are many resources you can use to find information, such as books, newspapers, magazines, and people. You can also use **electronic media,** which include things such as audiotapes, videotapes, films, and computers. CD-ROM encyclopedias and the Internet are two ways to gather information using a computer.

Directions: Review the list of resources that give information about guinea pigs. Use the list to tell which resource you would choose for each situation described on the next page.

Books *(Nonfiction)*
Guinea Pigs: How to Care for Them,
Feed Them, and Understand Them
by Katrin Behrend
I Love Guinea Pigs by Dick King-Smith
The Guinea Pig, An Owner's Guide by
Audrey Pavia

Books *(Fiction)*
Bedtime by Kate Duke
Olga De Polga by Michael Bond

Organizations
Guinea Pig Adoption Network
Home for Unwanted and Abandoned
Guinea Pigs

Internet Web Pages
Todd's Guinea Pig Hutch
Carlo's Guinea Pig Site

Internet Mailing Lists*
Gpigs

Internet Newsgroups*
Pets: Guinea Pigs

Internet Sound Files*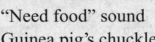
"Need food" sound
Guinea pig's chuckle

Videos
Pocket Pet Series Featuring: Guinea
Pigs

CD-ROMs
The ABC's of Caring for a Guinea Pig

*Mailing lists and newsgroups are discussions conducted on the Internet. People post questions and answers about a specific topic. You automatically receive mailing list posts in e-mail. You have to go to a newsgroup site to read news posted by other members of the newsgroup. An Internet sound file is a short audio recording of a specific sound. You can save the file and play the sound over and over again.

1. You are giving a presentation on guinea pigs to your class. You want to let students know how to adopt a guinea pig.

_____

_____

2. Also as part of your presentation, you want the class to hear the sound guinea pigs make when they are hungry.

_____

_____

3. You are interested in receiving information through e-mail about the care of guinea pigs.

_____

_____

4. Your class is creating a Web page about your class pet—a guinea pig named Honey. You are responsible for finding out what kinds of information you should include in a web page.

_____

_____

5. Choose one of the electronic media resources from the list. Give an example of a research project where a student might use this resource. Tell why this resource best suits the purposes of the project.

_____

_____

_____

_____

Notes for Home: Your child chose resources for completing projects. *Home Activity:* Visit a library with your child. Many libraries have media centers that provide public access to electronic media. Discuss the resources available and how your child might use them for study or research.

© Scott Foresman 4